Praise for Josh Brazier

"Meeting Josh during my time in a residential treatment program was a turning point in my life. At fourteen, I couldn't see my potential or all that the world had to offer. Josh helped me build confidence in who I am, encouraged me to try new things, and guided me in creating plans to be more active and social. Thanks to his mentorship, I now feel empowered and fulfilled in my life. The positive changes and plans we've worked on together have truly stuck, and my life continues to improve every day."

—**Ethan F.**

"Josh helped me understand what kind of man I want to be. And he taught me about good music, too. And cars. He took me to art films and concerts and college tours and rides in his El Camino. He thought he was *sooo* cool. And he was. Josh introduced me to the idea of a career in advertising, which is what I do now for work. And in seventeen years, he's never ignored my call!"

—**Will E.**

"I have known Josh for half of my life, and in that entire time he has been a constant source of guidance and wisdom. Josh has been one of my greatest friends and I feel forever grateful that he is in my life."

—**Nick A.**

"Josh's teachings have profoundly changed my perspective on life. His guidance in choosing a school and learning essential life skills has been invaluable. He has had a huge positive impact on my life through his mentorship."

—**Finn C.**

"Josh has been an incredible friend and mentor to me for many years. He has helped me work through a lot of issues that held me back in my life and I can honestly say I wouldn't be where I am today without the wisdom that Josh has imparted on me. Josh has always known exactly where and how to push me, but he's never pushed too far. Josh is also incredibly persistent and doesn't give up even when I do. I've had so many therapist and mental health professionals throughout my life, but none of them have been able to pinpoint exactly what I need like Josh has. I feel so incredibly lucky to know Josh and to have had the experiences I've had with him. His coaching and mentorship have truly been invaluable in helping me find myself and my path in life."

—Gordon C.

"In my darkest days I was closed off and unreceptive to help. Josh's methods reached me when others could not. His deep empathy and understanding of the human condition, born from a life of service and charity, were a lighthouse. Josh gave me a mental toolbox that allowed me not only to turn my life around, but to maintain my trajectory through heartbreak, illness, and injury. I would not be where I am today without him."

—Dr. Cole Woodland

"This man is a true angel on earth. He has been a bright guiding light for my family and I for over a decade...he became my older brother's mentor at a time when things seemed dark. Little did I know Josh would open our hearts to the beauty of humanitarian service by visiting orphanages in Mexico, India, and Africa. I would not be the person I am today without him. His impact on my family has been such a blessing."

—Angelica E.

"Josh is an angel for our family and I suspect for countless others. His guidance and support for my three children since 2011 continues to uplift and inspire us to live a better life where compassion is second nature."

—Carmen E.

"Our son journeyed to Africa and India with Josh and five other boys and lived for six weeks in orphanages. He came home driven academically and athletically. He came home a man. Josh continues to be in our lives and, more importantly, in Finn's. Their relationship and the impact it has had have been beyond our most optimistic expectations. Most easily put: A+"

—Tim C.

"I'll never forget that one time in Mexico when I was helping an orphanage with a group of students. It was late on one of the final nights outside Ensenada and Josh decided it might be a good idea to pick up a pizza. He must have been quite tired, because one of my earliest memories of our friendship is Josh sprawled out on his bed with nothing to accompany him but a steamy box of cheese pie. I have reminded Josh of this memory during virtually every single one of our subsequent conversations. As strange as it sounds, I don't believe our friendship of seventeen years could have prospered quite the way it did had it not been for that pizza. It signified the beginning of an everlasting string of late-night phone calls and texts with Josh typically saying, 'let's get creative.' And we would. We would figure out a plan to put me back on track in an out-of-the-box way. During our numerous adventures around the world and countless conversations, Josh has given me the tools I need to look at problems differently and solve them creatively. And to think, it all started with a pizza in Mexico."

—Brad A.

"Josh Brazier has been an awesome mentor and friend to me throughout the years. He has helped me to dig deep into who I am and what I want out of life. Often asking questions that I didn't know how to answer. He is very charitable, humble, and has a heart of gold. I have been very blessed to have known Josh in my life and very grateful to be able to call him my friend."

—Cameron A.

MAKING PLANS THAT STICK

Books by Josh Brazier

Bang Head Here: A Guide to Reconnecting and Communicating with Your Loved Ones (2022)

MAKING PLANS THAT STICK

An Honest Look at the Mindsets That Keep Us Stuck

by Josh Brazier

mango
PUBLISHING

Miami, FL

For permission requests, please contact the publisher at:
Mango Publishing Group
5966 South Dixie Highway, Suite 300
Miami, FL 33143
info@mango.bz

For special orders, quantity sales, course adoptions and corporate sales, please email the publisher at sales@mango.bz. For trade and wholesale sales, please contact Ingram Publisher Services at customer.service@ingramcontent.com or +1.800.509.4887.

Making Plans That Stick: An Honest Look at the Mindsets that Keep Us Stuck

Library of Congress Cataloging-in-Publication number: 2024938787
ISBN: (p) 978-1-68481-621-7 (e) 978-1-68481-622-4
BISAC category code YAN011000, YOUNG ADULT NONFICTION / Careers

For Carlos and Ivan
Thanks for getting me back on track

TABLE OF CONTENTS

A NOTE TO THE READER

Dear Hopeful Planner,

I have struggled; I've also lived well. What follows is me exploring how I went from being stuck in many ways to having my plans stick.

I like to tell stories. I like to teach through stories and examples. So that's how I decided to approach this book: stories, suggestions, insights, exercises, questions, skills, tools—they are all in here. I didn't just want to say, "Hey, you, take these steps, and all will be well" (there are plenty of books like that out there!), so you'll notice *Making Plans That Stick* is both a reflection on my experiences and a how-to guide.

You'll find some stories dispersed throughout the book—until you reach Part 4. Then it's all stories. These narratives are meant to inspire and illuminate the concepts discussed.

Together, we will:

- Assess

- Create

- Do

- and, most importantly, Be(come).

But this *has* to be personal because our plans for ourselves are deeply personal—that much I came to realize while I was writing. I can and will throw out concepts left and right on these pages, but I need you to see yourself in them, struggling with them like I did, and succeeding with them like I have.

Have fun working out your own versions of the concepts, exercises, and skills I suggest. You make them real by making them yours.

You matter. Your plans matter.

This is real life.

This whole process will be super meaningful if you let it play out. Let it play out.

—JOSH

Introduction

TOO LATE?

Courtesy of the Kaiizen Foundation

Starting to Kaiizen

As the fire died down and I adjusted my sleeping bag, I think that's when it all hit me. I was on a beach in Mexico, surrounded by sixty of my good friends. Tents were scattered on the sand like the stars in the sky, which were amazing and bright that night. I had just finished up some conversations about what we had just accomplished. My fellow planners and I doused the fire and decided to go get warm in our sleeping bags and turn in for the night. It all seemed like an important moment.

I was exhausted; we'd pulled off a sort of miracle, and as I lay there, I had no clue what to make of it all.

I felt grounded and lost—a weird contradiction. A contradiction that will come up a lot for all of us in life. We all want things for ourselves, whether simple or grand. Those wants create expectations, high hopes, desire, and sometimes deep suffering when things don't go as planned. Weirdly, we can feel both at peace and anxious about our future selves and plans. Totally scared, too, just like I was that night on the beach in Mexico. Because we all have these moments we experience when life really doesn't feel the same afterward. It was for sure one of those moments for me. Wanting more for yourself and your plans might feel the same as it did for me: a pivotal moment when you decide you could do things differently, that you want your life to be different, even though you know it will be complicated and full of challenges.

As I was settling in that night on the beach, I was looking for some context for all these contradictory feelings. I reflected on a time when I felt similarly, and my thoughts drifted to another transformative moment. I found similar feelings when I graduated from high school. I was surprised then at how things just changed and shifted so much and so rapidly, overnight. The graduation ceremony blew by, followed by the fun and exhausting graduation party. I woke up the morning after graduation, and everything and everyone had changed. Friends left for their summer programs, and all of a sudden, my parents were on me to get a real summer job. I remember thinking, am I even ready for this? Suddenly, with all its drama and schoolwork, high school was more appealing to me than what lay ahead. I felt excited and hopeful, yet scared and unsure of myself. As I reflected, all snug in my sleeping bag, I finally was able to lock onto what I was truly feeling the day after I graduated from high school: I was in charge of my plans and my success. The structures and scaffolding that had propped me up to that point were no longer there. Life was on me, and I struggled to accept it.

It is a decision we all need to make; the earlier, the better. Accept that it is scary when we hold the reins, when we are in the driver's seat, solo, planning our route and driving each mile. It was a powerful connection I made on the beach that evening. This thing we had started in Mexico had been given a life of its own, and we were now stewards of it, fully in charge of its destiny. It was going to be unknown, exciting, and very scary. I accepted it all that night as you will have to eventually with your plans, hopes, and dreams. It will be a road with many twists and turns.

A bit of that fear of the unknown still lingered in the pit of my stomach that night on the beach. I still doubted myself. I tossed and turned a bit. What had we done? Yes, we had successfully road-tripped sixty-three people eight hundred miles one way with only one crazy volunteer arrested (yikes!). We'd gotten twenty cars over the border, and we'd only really lost one of these cars for a few hours in Mexico (scary!). Quite the feat. And yes, I admit, my cherished VW van broke down in Las Vegas; and later, while driving ole Red, a friend swiped my beloved van with an equally red fire hydrant (sad!). Someone had also run over my surfboards (!!!) in the parking lot while we were loading them on the old VW. Dozens of other crazy things happened to us in Mexico on that trip, but we all pushed through; we were all just stoked to be there and were having the time of our lives. We surfed, ate yummy tacos, and hung out with forty of the most incredible kids at the orphanage where we had just volunteered our blood, sweat, and literal tears. At times, it was a total nightmare. The level of anxiety my friends and I felt as we labored minute by minute to carry out the plans we'd made was palpable. We wanted everyone to have a good time. We wanted things to work out. We had spent days and days thinking through what could go wrong. None of what we imagined could go wrong did, but some very real surprises came our way. We had to pivot, think on our feet, and not give up. We couldn't let our emotions or fears guide us. We believed in our plans. And as I finally fell asleep that last night on the beach, I had a huge smile. We had pulled it off! Our plans mostly stuck, and as we built our nonprofit from the ground up, I became familiar with the concepts and ideas that helped our plans stick.

Courtesy of the Kaiizen Foundation

Starting to Wing It

The eight hundred miles back home at 60–65 mph gave us time to think. Long uphills slowed ole Red down to 45–50 mph, and without AC in my van, the journey was long, hot, and sweaty. We were all joking and happy, hot but content.

You see, it was just six or so weeks before that last night on the beach in Mexico that we even started making solid plans for the trip. We didn't have the time to make epic and detailed plans. We had full credit loads, part-time jobs, and the like. To be honest, that was a good thing. Overthinking will kill your plans before they even start.

Just two months earlier, three close friends and I had raised a little bit of money to take a scouting mission to Baja California. We drove all night after our evening college classes to barely arrive in time to tour an orphanage in Mexico the next day. We drove into the unknown. But a key ingredient to making our plans stick was there: **we had a vision that was meaningful, and we sensed adventure in our plans.**

The Why

Before we move on with the story, I need to stop and emphasize this.

This book will not be a prototypical exploration of plans, goals, habits, etc. Why? Because, when you face the inevitable challenge to your plans, it might be hard to remember the process or concept needed to get you through. But you will remember stories and how they made you feel, and as you look back over what you remember about a particular story, you will naturally connect with what to do and how to move forward. It is just how we humans work. We are a storytelling species. Stories teach and stories stick.

On that exploratory trip to Baja, we really had no clue what we were doing. We truly had a blank sheet of paper in front of us. That blank white page did not scare us. We had a pencil with an eraser. When we messed up, we erased, learned the lesson, and moved forward. Nothing had to be perfect. Why? Because our vision for what we were doing was more important than our perfectionism and pride. Our plans were an adventure. We wanted to help, and to help people help more. Our plans were based on good intentions, as yours will need to be, and we were willing to get through the hard times because our vision for what it could become inspired and guided us.

You may think this is incredibly different from your plans to just be consistent and get to the gym every day, but these efforts aren't too far off.

Your *Why* for your plans needs to be set before your first step. Your *Why* will be the gas in your tank. Our *Why*, this desire to help young people find an outlet for their creativity and energy, was present through every pivot and disaster on that first trip to Mexico. It kept us going. It kept us learning.

Luckily, everything went as planned on that scouting mission. As we drove home, full of tacos and love for all these kids we just met, and with sand still on our feet, we started brainstorming what we could do next. We quickly realized that we hadn't asked any good questions; we hadn't really taken any notes. We had just played with the kids and bonded with them. That proved to be key. We fell in love with our *Why* while playing soccer, arm wrestling, and pushing kids on swings. On that drive back, we realized we hadn't figured out any of the logistics at all.

Where would we get food? Water? We knew where we would sleep, but how could we ensure that we had the supplies and activities to pull off another great trip? That was the plan, you see, to head back to our colleges and announce that, in about six to eight weeks, we'd be taking a group to the orphanage in Mexico to play, fix up the place, and experience Mexican culture and hospitality.

Our college had three or four universities nearby. College students have plenty of creativity, some time, and tons of energy. There seemed to be an energy after the tragic 2004 tsunami: everyone was looking for ways to give back and lend a hand. Our *Why* was to fill that need. Previously, my friends and I had thrown some fun benefit concerts and raised some decent money to support tsunami victims, but we just kept hearing from people that they were looking for something more meaningful. That's why we took that exploratory trip to meet the kids at that orphanage in Baja California. On the drive home, we had that blank piece of paper and twelve hours ahead of us. So, we got to work throwing around and putting to paper ideas that could work to help us solve our *Why*.

This was 2005 (I am not so young now, mind you), so communicating via text message was not easy and each text cost money to send or receive. Google wasn't even a popular thing yet. The internet wasn't the resource it is today. We had to make actual phone calls. We relied on people and their advice. And more importantly, we trusted in what they were saying. Hint: you will need to do the same with me here. I fear that, when making your plans, you will have access to way too much information and it will paralyze you. When we went scouting in Baja, we printed out directions; we had to find guideposts and stop and ask people for help when we got lost. Another hint: please be open to being a little old-school in this process. A lot of what I am going to suggest will get you offline and away from technology and into the real and vulnerable world.

That text I sent on my Nokia phone after that scouting trip was simple: *Meet up at my apartment at six p.m. on Sunday, we are planning a trip to an orphanage in Mexico.*

That was it.

Sixty-three people showed up to that first meeting, and soon we found out that our Why was real and it gave us a huge boost of confidence. The day after that meeting, we began planning trip details while cramming for midterms and writing papers. We had no clue what we were doing, but I think we felt we wanted to show up somehow and meet the moment. We kept writing ideas down on that sheet of paper, and while some stuck, most were either quickly erased or just laughed at (what were we thinking?), but we kept at it. We got our professors involved. We tapped into the energy of those sixty-three people. Weeks flew by, and soon, it was four in the morning, and we had twenty cars packed and ready to charge down to Baja. At some point, it will be the same for you and your plans: you will need to get into the car and go, to try. Even though the following four days were insanity, they got us started. It is time we get started.

Meeting Moments

It might be why you have this book in your hand right now. There might be some moments in your life that need to be met, and you are probably feeling like I did all those years ago. *Can I do this? Are my future plans worth the risk? Am I even ready for this?* Or maybe you are feeling like I did on the beach: *What should I even do?*

I will tell you how easy it is to get paralyzed in these pivotal moments of transition to different stages of life that feel so meaningful. Those fears, doubts, and concerns snowball, and we can find ourselves beyond stuck.

This book's title is so simple; it's on purpose. While we were cruising slowly back from Mexico in the hot California desert, I had to make some personal decisions. I was truly feeling stuck, unsure how to proceed. Driving at sixty miles per hour with a gnawing in the pit of your stomach for eight hundred miles is painful. A lot had gone right, but I needed to take all the mistakes and screw-ups we had all just experienced and learn how to make better plans, and then I needed to learn how to follow through much better. I felt that the kids at the orphanage were counting on us, and little did I know that thousands of future volunteers were as well. The future is always bright, unknown, and super scary, but ultimately, it is ours to determine, craft, and fight for. I just wanted whatever we came up with to really stick, to be meaningful.

This book is about my fight to get there. Ultimately, these lives we want to create, these ideas we have for ourselves, are worth fighting for.

Our plans will truly stick *if* we want to fight for them. The lessons from my experiences leading up to that first trip to Mexico are clear: **Know your why, know nothing will go exactly as planned, enjoy all the pivots (pivots are lessons to be learned), but don't quit on your plans, and remember that plans that stick have flexibility built in.**

Do me a favor, right here, right now. As you read through this book, I'm going to ask you to pause at certain points and engage directly with exercises and reflections. Not later, but now. In the very moment, as the stories and lessons are present, your mind is opening up. Take these actions immediately as you encounter them, allowing the experience to resonate more deeply.

Your Ideal Why

I want you to grab a blank piece of paper. I want you to grab a pencil. I don't want you to hold back. I just want you to jot down your most ideal, wonderful, and inspiring ideas around your *Why*s, your plans, your goals, your thoughts about what could be. There are no bad ideas in brainstorming, and that is all this is: a chance to unashamedly get some ideas on paper, the beginnings of a vision for your next steps.

Please know as well that I acknowledge that you may be in a low place right now. You may laugh at this and question why this exercise is necessary. I get that. But please try. You can start by writing, *I have no clue.* Great! We got something down. It's okay not to have a clue. (I have had no clue hundreds of times in my life.) It is also okay to want to be the next Steve Jobs or Taylor Swift. Write it down.

Next, jot down some expectations that others have for you right now. Schooling. A job. Moving out. Feel the weight of those. They may be your current reality, and that is okay too. It can feel like a lot of pressure.

Focus on one. Let's say getting a job. I want you to take it one step further right now. We will get into other exercises as this book progresses, but for now, write down one idea around a job that could be meaningful. Let's not fight the idea of a job; let's just see if there's a job that could feel meaningful, like "I'd like to work around animals." Find that little nugget and write it down. It is there. If it doesn't feel like it is, then that is the fight we are in! To find those meaningful nuggets. There are ideas within you that beg to be discovered, and they are worth fighting your mind and all its tricks (we will learn more about these soon). Just because it is hard now doesn't mean we give up. Remember, these ideas aren't permanent; they are a starting point.

Maybe

Maybe you hate the fact that you even have to read a book like this right now.

I get it. You feel put in the spotlight by others, maybe backed into a corner. People are expecting things from you, and you don't quite feel you've got your feet under you. Maybe you've failed a couple few times, came home early from college, or lost your first job. You feel trapped, mad, maybe a little scared.

Or maybe you are not motivated at all. Nothing about how this world works seems to make sense to you, and you don't see the point in it all.

Maybe you might have jumped through every hoop out there—high school, college, jobs—and things still aren't working out for you. You did what you were told, and you don't feel you have a lot to show for it.

Maybe your family situation is not ideal, there isn't the support that most get, and you feel all too alone in this process.

I admit that I don't know fully what it is like to walk in your specific shoes. Culture, nationality, race, religion, education, personal identities, and society at large all impose their ideals, pressures, and expectations, whether correct or not.

Maybe you are finally gaining some momentum, and this book, whether given to you or bought by you, was chosen for a little boost. Maybe it is a little of this and a little of that. I think it's that way for all of us.

No matter how you got to this page, I get you. I don't know you, but in a very real way, I do.

You see, this book is about transformation, but not in the way you might think. I do not deal in fantasy or hyperbole. I will not promise you that, by reading this book, all will magically be right and well. Honestly, this book is about the *work* you'll need to put in to make your plans stick.

This is also the part of the book where I try to set the hook. I gotta give you a reason to keep going, to trust me. I don't want to waste your time. You need to know that.

I want you to be skeptical. I want you to wrestle with the concepts in this book. If you do, that means you are making them real. You are trying to figure out how they fit. You are applying them to your specific situation and seeing where things land. More of that, please! Yes, to all of it. But let me say that I don't want the skepticism to keep you from trying. From doing the work, deliberately and consistently. Nothing happens overnight, and your true skepticism should be directed toward your mind and the many, many excuses and complaints it will make as you apply what we are talking about here. In our hyper-novel culture, it seems the first habit I need to break is for you to even think that the fruits of labor come fast. They don't. I am sorry, but don't give up on me yet. We've just become so very used to everything happening quickly. True change isn't always quick.

Every story, insight, and piece of advice I give here is from the very struggle I am asking you to engage in.

This is truly the best of me to this date on these pages.

I'm going to tell stories, share the lessons, then give you some steps to take, some advice to wrestle with, and some action items to make it all real and lasting.

My experiences and stories span decades, continents, and tens of thousands of hours mentoring. I have been given a window into the lives of many of you, but not all of you. Your mind will try to dismiss what I am saying because I might not get it perfectly tuned to your own life and situation. Please be patient with me. My intention is to make it all real for you, but part of your work is to apply what I am saying to your specific situation while trying not to over-personalize the advice. There are always pathways forward. Always. They all require effort to apply to our current needs and I would appreciate trust in that as we move forward together.

My life has been spent observing. Listening. I get the calls from you at two in the morning when all feels lost. None of the advice, formulas, skills, or stories that follow are fake. They come from hard-won relationships I created with folks from all walks of life, in dozens and dozens of countries, that I have worked alongside. I don't say worked *with*; I truly mean *alongside*. I learn while I coach and mentor. I see patterns, I take risks, and I make mistakes. Most importantly, though, I invest in my tribe. You are now part of that tribe.

I did have people invest in me at certain pivotal moments in my life. As I write this, I imagine those people and the moments attached to them and feel strongly I can do the same for you. I want to be that person for you.

By giving this book a chance, you are giving me a chance. I have a lot to prove to you.

We already got started. I hope you still have that piece of paper in front of you. I hope you have taken some time to jot down some plans, any plans. I want to use those ideas while we talk here. I want you to take those ideas and pass them through the advice and insights I give here. You may have written: hike more, learn ballet, or get into shape. You may have jotted down: get out of this city, or out of this relationship, or out of this job. Those are great too. We are setting a vision, and you need that vision, or the start of one, to make this book make sense.

The diversity of our situations makes our stories unique, beautiful, and incredibly complicated. Remember, I do not dismiss or invalidate who you are or what you've experienced by sharing my life's path.

All I know is that I have struggled, wrestled, hurt deeply, and failed miserably many, many times in the soil of my own situation. I know that you have as well.

We don't have to put on a brave face. There are too many books out there that deal only in motivational ideas and possibly unrealistic growth and expectations.

Through my own struggles, I have come to value learning about and from what gets in the way of my success more than the actual results. That is where the work is, and that work is beautiful and why I believe we are here together. We learn from what is getting in our way; we don't want to become victims to it.

Let's start out with a personal story that will highlight my life's main struggle, where my learning has been most intense and difficult. I am not going to use names a lot in this book and will change some details just as a precaution, but remember, everything in these pages is real life, and the advice and steps I tie to each story are valuable and worth investing in.

So, follow along. We will dive into a story; laugh at my idiosyncrasies; learn some applicable concepts and skills; and then we will move on to another story, concept, or exercise. Rinse and repeat. Me being vulnerable all along the way so we can have some good lessons and things to discuss. Here we go.

Supergirl

There are those rare moments in life when things slow down and seem so much clearer. I was at a dance (yes, a dance), and from across the room, I spotted a blonde surfer girl wearing a Superman t-shirt. Maybe you are thinking right now: How old is this dude? A *dance*? Time slowing down? This guy has seen too many movies. Don't check out yet, please.

I got the guts to approach this girl and asked for a dance. We hit it off quickly, and I found myself falling a bit in love. She just had a cool vibe, and it was clear she knew who she was. When you are younger, that stands out. At that dance, there were like a billion of us playing to the crowd, acting cooler than we were, and trying to be so many things we were not. Supergirl wasn't.

Confidence is so, so attractive.

In the months that followed that dance, even though we lived some miles from each other, Supergirl and I got to know each other, and I thought we were developing into something fun and unique. We were, slowly, but it was feeling special.

We had quirky picnics on those landscaping islands between lanes on a major road, beach time, and other fun dates or hangouts. I was an idiot teenager. Insecure yet confident, bold in all the wrong ways, and insecure in all the typical ways, but what I loved about my time with Supergirl was how she made me feel. I wanted to get better. I wanted to be better. She had a vision for her life, and she stuck to it. I, on the other hand, was all over the place, but when I was with her, I felt more possible, more grounded. All the feels, you know?

I was falling hard, and yet, being the thick-headed idiot I am, I didn't always make the best decisions. I was learning how to put another person ahead of myself, no easy task at barely seventeen. We went to different schools, lived a bit of distance from each other, had jobs, lives, family, sports, and all the typical teenage drama.

At the time, I was working at a local Mexican dive restaurant. I ate more chips on any given day than we served to customers. I remember one Friday evening, I had plans to see Supergirl before she left for a long trip in her classic old car. I was at work when she called to firm up our plans. I was tired. My friends were all hanging out. Spending time with Supergirl meant driving thirty miles after work. I hesitated. She noticed, the drama increased, and I ended up canceling the plans. I went, hung out with my friends, a little mad at myself and kind of sick to my stomach that I'd let her down because I was lazy, that I feared missing out on what my friends were doing more, and the like. It was an immature move, and I knew I had not only made her mad, but disappointed her, because we were building something together.

Saturday came and went. She was on her trip, and we didn't have cell phones then. I'd have to patch things up when she got back. That was my hope. Senior year had just started, and life would be busy until I got a call from her.

The call I got Sunday morning was not the one I expected. My parents yelled up the stairs that I had a call from a friend. I picked up, and my friend told me Supergirl had been killed on her trip in a head-on collision with a semitruck. Life slowed down again, even more, and in dramatic fashion, all the details my friend was giving me felt like another language. I sort of just slid down the wall into a seated position in total shock. I thanked my friend for letting me know, hung up, and then it hit me.

Supergirl, this amazing girl, that blonde surfer girl in a Superman T-shirt, left this world mad at me—even worse, disappointed in me. This girl who made me feel secure and want to do better was gone.

Arrested Development

I don't tell that story very often. I think, in some ways, I don't want to admit what an impact it had on me. I am a pretty solid person, but when I think of that time, I just lose my ground. It is one of those sacred but formative life experiences we all have. It is one I have had to work through and understand, and with help from professionals, friends, and just sitting with it, I've come to learn just how impactful it was for me.

You see, I have never been good at long-term relationships, or at least I never thought I was. I was always a little off in that department, to be honest. I had developed some strong ways to protect myself after my experience with Supergirl. Her story was very much out of my control—at least parts weren't, I guess—but soon after her passing, I developed this need to be able to control all the outcomes in my life, or I would not try at all. Suddenly, I couldn't stand the thought that someone was upset with me, or feeling like I could let someone down. My personality was changing, and the parts of me that needed help became amplified. I started to obsess internally and go out of my way to make things right if I felt I'd wronged someone. The guilt was intense. I would over-plan and overthink, hoping things would turn out right. With time, I found I could control these fears by always being helpful to others and putting myself last. It was a part of me that was already there, but my experience with Supergirl just exacerbated it. I was always a good and creative leader, but the fears that were planted with my experience with her turned those positive qualities into a whole other animal.

Try as I might, I would get into a relationship and suffocate it with my fears and insecurities. Way in the back of my mind, I had a little itch that always needed to be scratched. It was the thought, "What if it all happens again?"

My ability to develop healthily in relationships was arrested. Stopped. I didn't realize it for years or through many, many failed relationships. I was stuck, lost, a bit clueless, but feeling like a total failure while all my friends around me were getting married, starting their families, and finding that person who made them want to get better.

The narrative I created in my mind was simply "I am not good at relationships," and after I spent a while trying, I gave up.

Arrested development. Completely.

Big Ts and Little ts

I realize not everyone has had the same experience I had with Supergirl. It was a formative moment, a big T for me during a very tumultuous time (high school). I was finding out who I was and with all the hormones, decisions being made about the future, and voices swirling around in my head, I was lucky things didn't turn out worse.

I am going to take a small pause here. Trauma is a big word. It does get thrown around a lot these days. It has taken on meanings, importance, and weight at times that the word never intended for itself. It is a uniquely personal word because, truly, we can only define for ourselves what is a big T or a little t, or even a t at all. Other people will try to mold our traumas or define them for us. It can get more than confusing. Ts are for trusted people, no matter how big or small they are, and they are meant to be processed and, with time and healing, released.

We are, and we are not, simultaneously, our traumas. They build us, destroy us, confuse us, while at the same time showing us new perspectives and giving us deep and profound insights about our lives—also ways to improve and heal. It's all so confusing, it's no wonder we are all arrested in some way in our development. Starting new things feels impossible when we feel so stuck in so many places.

We are sorting through this life with half the playbook when we are unaware of these arrested parts of ourselves. We may know what is arrested, or we may not. The only thing we really feel is like I have for all these years, like a failure. It didn't matter how much success I found in other places; where my development was arrested was all I could see. I sat daily in amazing meetings building amazing programs, I traveled the world and changed many lives, and yet I would go home, and I was alone.

I had to start to understand all my little ts and Big Ts, any trauma really, as I defined and felt them. I had to see where my healthy development had stalled. It felt daunting, but it seemed to be the only place where I could start.

So, in this book, that is where we will start too. Because I fully believe we can heal from all our Big Ts and little ts.

So, let's start. I am going to give you a journaling exercise right now. It will help us when we get to Part 1: Assess. There, we will begin to unpack your memories and their messages to us, but first we need to break the ice.

I broke the ice with my story about Supergirl. It was difficult for me to write. To this day, I struggle with long-term relationships, but my plans around that part of my life, as you will see, are shaping up and sticking better. I am not writing this book from atop a pedestal, looking down at you. I am in the thick of it too. I have good days and bad days. What is different now is that I have this process I am taking you through to use daily, and it helps keep me pointed in the right direction.

So, grab a journal and some paper, and sit with this one set of questions. Think about it. Feel the feelings and emotions around it. Then take the time to really write about it. To really explore whether you are ready to move forward.

Are there parts of me whose development is arrested?

Can I admit it? See it? Am I at all familiar with what is arrested in my life?

Even if it is a small act, right now, like writing *yes* in the margin of this book, then we have made a huge stride forward, for most of us, to be honest, don't want to look at these parts of ourselves, ever.

If you feel open to it, feel free to write down the parts of you that you feel are arrested right now. No need to get into the weeds. You can write:

- Career
- Relationships
- My relationship with shame or guilt

Any part of you that feels stalled. No more journaling is needed, just acknowledgment. I want you to be aware of these parts of you as you begin to make your plans. Awareness is key, and you'll see the mindsets created by these arrested parts of ourselves at work over time. They'll try to sabotage your plans, but you'll see them coming, quicker and quicker, and you'll use your skills more effectively with each passing day.

But let's get into another fun story about fully owning your diverse and wonderfully complicated story.

Courtesy of the Kaiizen Foundation

You and Your Story

While in India, I was giving a workshop to a couple dozen high-school-aged young men. Awesome kids, hungry for a good life and opportunities. I had a great workshop planned. I was going to teach them that their life was a story, and they knew what made a good story. They knew what made a good character. If you've ever been to a movie theater in India, you'd know. They take their movies seriously and their heroes even more seriously. The workshop was going to be a slam dunk.

It was.

Afterward, the young men came up and asked the usual questions. What should I do about my education? How did you know what you wanted to do? I answered and nailed it all again. The energy in the room was good, and I went back to where I was staying and took a rest from the hot and humid Indian summer.

That night I would see the young men again for dinner and a bonfire. It wasn't easy to take a nap in that heat, but I needed one.

Dinner with the boys was spicy and the conversation was light and fun. We went up to the roof of a building in the complex we were staying at and started a bonfire. The questions commenced, and I was ready. Everything started out well, but then Prasanth made a bomb of a statement: "Josh, I loved your workshop, but it was not real. You come from America. I am in India. I am competing with a billion other people who want what I want and what you already have. There's no way it is as simple as you say it was."

Mic drop, right onto my foot.

I froze. I was young! I was trying to inspire! I thought I had done a good job, but after Prasanth spoke, the others chimed in with their own true, real stories. The reality was that they weren't living easy lives. I listened, put myself in their shoes, and really sat with them as they told their stories and expressed their fears. I heard them. We stayed up way too late as we discussed real life, real stories. It was incredible but difficult. I am sure it would be the same if you and I had a chance to really speak.

I try to learn every day. I make mistakes, often, on the daily. I had a blind spot exposed to me that day, and it is something I am bringing up now to you. The advice and the tools I will lay out in this book are not one-size-fits-all, but the foundations of them are true. They will work. In a way, I am not reinventing the wheel; I just found a better way to use it.

That night, those boys and I reached that understanding. I couldn't change their poverty, their family situations, or their class, but I tried that night by the bonfire to customize my best-learned advice to their individual stories.

You have your unique story. I want to help you understand it and sift through it. That's number one for me. Without that step, us assessing, we won't get very far. You are going to have to get comfortable sitting in the mud with me for a while. But we have to start with what is getting in the way. No piece of advice will get beyond your own unique roadblocks and hurdles.

As I mentioned, there is no one on this planet who doesn't have some form of arrested development. For you it might be something around academics, your social life, relationships, your family, your future—the list could go on. You may feel stuck, like a failure, that things are just not working out. I get that. It is something I feel every day. These are not comfortable feelings to sit in. No matter what you are facing, there is hope. You might not see yourself in the stories I share, but the concepts all relate to each other, and I know you will relate to them. It is a case of same problem/different problem. Things might not look the same on the outside, but we are all struggling in some fashion to make our plans stick. Don't let your mind grab onto one detail when trying to relate to someone or a story. That is your mind playing tricks; it is a distraction, often an excuse, and a path to being victim to our individual stories. We tend to say, "Oh, that's not me" or "That's not real, so it doesn't relate." Not true. Same story/different story. Don't get lost in my details. Look for the concept and find how it all relates to the details of your life. It's there.

You see, from my experience with Supergirl grew outrageous perfectionism; it was already in me to a degree, but that experience sent it to a whole other level, especially when it came to relationships. For a while, I stopped attempting anything I couldn't be super good at, including relationships. When I started to see that I did a really good job at helping other people, I focused on developing into this person who people would go to for help of all kinds. I got my validation or dopamine hits from those successes and my life took off in a whole other direction. I think you can relate.

Where you are now is probably not where you hoped you'd end up. Nothing is permanent—find some hope in that statement. As we progress along in this book together, you will unarrest your development, get creative with new plans, and learn how to follow through, and ultimately become the person you want to be, over time, with lots of trial and error and patience. That is why I set this book up this way. It is a way of being just as much as it is a process.

Once this slightly long introduction (sorry!!!) concludes, we are going to dive into the four parts of this book. As I mentioned earlier, we will learn to

1. Assess
2. Create
3. Do
4. Be(come)

I will help you get to know how we got to where we are and give you some concepts and tools to get to the source of things that are arresting our development. Then I want to help you think differently, get creative, and find some ways to experiment with new paths, hobbies, and ideas. You'll learn to get creative with your own life again or for the first time; you'll also stop comparing yourself to others so that you can find your own way out of your own mess and into something more fitted to you and your values.

Do, or practicing, deliberately, is one of the greatest things I can teach you. My job over the last couple of decades has basically been a form of exposure therapy. I help people do things. I've learned many best practices to try, to stick with, so you can learn to love the things you do in this life. Please take seriously all that we will go through in the parts where we assess and create. We need that strong foundation in order for Do and Be to make sense.

Listen, I have learned that at the end of this thing we call life, it matters very little what we've accomplished. No one remembers that stuff, really. They will remember and feel who you were more than any other thing. Your being, your energy, your essence, or whatever woo-woo word you want to use, will stick with them. When I think of Supergirl now, or anyone else I've lost, I rarely think of a specific memory; I feel how they made me feel. So, as we unarrest our development, please know, we are working toward that kind of life, one where you are happy with who you are, with what you will be to others. Those are the foundational plans I want to have stick in your life.

So let me introduce a formula I try to live by daily.

The Hope Formula

Deliberate practice + sense of accomplishment = hope

I came up with this simple formula when I was struggling to make little parts of my plan stick. Remember, I deal with insane perfectionism, to the point where I would quit far too soon because I was worried I wouldn't succeed or be able to fully control the outcome. You'll see this play out in some upcoming stories.

I wanted to introduce this formula now because, just as with admitting that we have some arrested development going on in our lives, I wanted to show you from the get-go that there was another side to the coin I called perfectionism/control.

The Formula in Action

After not following through for the millionth time on going to the gym, I just felt I was destined to be in okay shape for the rest of my life. The gym wasn't doing it for me. I'd show up, work a few machines, do cardio until my brain convinced me not to, and then get in the car to drive home, feeling like a failure. There was no passion in my actions at the gym, no deliberateness. Was I there to practice using those machines? Was there a better way for me to practice moving my body? Maybe, if I had the passion to use those machines long enough, I would have been rewarded with the sense of accomplishment needed to keep going and improve. It was on that millionth car ride home when I realized I wanted to practice something deliberately and long enough so I could get that feeling of accomplishment. As I drove, I felt something new, different, around my health and exercise. I felt hope.

I started brainstorming ways I liked moving my body. Hiking, swimming, yoga, to name a few. I decided to stick with those. To not exercise in a way that wasn't congruent to me. And I started practicing those things. I started feeling good about those things. I live with a lot of hope now due to those things I deliberately practice. You will too.

We know this; we are what we do, what we think, what we eat—you've heard all those things. Let me simplify it again: we are what we practice. If we practice good things, we will get a nice hit of dopamine, or a sense of accomplishment, and if you really think about it, the main feeling a sense of accomplishment gives us is hope. It's the feeling that we can go another day, improve a little more, or get to where we want to go. Unfortunately, as in my case, it goes both ways. We can practice negative habits, grab onto defeating thoughts, and then look for ways to justify those habits and thoughts. It is a cycle. But we can still get validated for it, and then that hit of dopamine that says *you suck*, or *you are worthless*, or all the other crazy and harsh stories we can tell about ourselves, builds the way we see the world and how we show up.

Practice good things, and if you feel stuck, like you can't drop a bad habit, please know there is always another side to a coin.

The Other Side of the Coin

I quickly learned that every coin has two sides as I was sitting in my own mess. If I was sitting on a particular day in some negative emotion, say shame, with effort I could find the opposite emotion (worthiness) and invest in it as my way out in that moment. Say I was feeling shameful because I felt like I let someone down and couldn't help them (this is a feeling I often feel). My mind would race, trying to find a way to solve or to make things right, often to control how someone felt about me. Remember, with Supergirl, she left this world not too happy with me, and this created a huge need to make people happy with me for fear it would repeat. I got better at catching what I was feeling, which we will dive into later, and when I did, I would realize I needed pure, no-strings-attached connection with someone safe. It would make me feel worthy again when I did. So, I would call a grandparent or sit in a memory of pure connection I had recently been in, and the shame would begin to melt. I would realize I wasn't a lost cause or hopeless. **I could always find the other side of the coin if I could label what I was truly feeling correctly.** That gave me huge amounts of hope. There is always another side of the coin to counterbalance what you are feeling. It is why I came up with all these formulas. I noticed that, just by acknowledging that there was an opposite emotion I could practice, I could create formulas and steps that I could repeat and hone. We will practice this more in the coming chapters, but practicing is key. Formulas give us steps with verifiable outcomes.

Quick Takeaway

Just as there are two sides to a coin, there's an opposite, more positive side to whatever struggle you are dealing with. If you can label what you are feeling, be bold and Google: what's the opposite of guilt?—(respect)—you'll find a place to start! You might intuitively feel what opposite action you should practice, but don't be afraid to look it up.

Practice the positive opposite of your negative feelings and you'll start to build some good momentum. Let me finally wrap up this introduction now.

Courtesy of the author

The Lineup

I used to surf a lot more than I do now. We will explore another one of my Big Ts around that later, but I wanted to share a visual with you as we close out the concepts in this introduction.

When you are sitting in the lineup, waiting for your chance, everything is totally unknown. The tides, wind, and sets all give you clues but, in a way, you are just sitting in the middle of the ocean amongst other people who are waiting for their chance too. Your hope is that a wave comes your way, and that when it does, you are in the best position, that you've practiced enough to take advantage of that wave, and that you will have a good enough experience to want to work your way back into the lineup after a nice little wave. That is what we are doing here. I want you to be ready when your wave comes. I have worked with thousands of people over my lifetime, trying to create momentum for them. Some of that has been in big groups, or through programs I have started or consulted on. But most of my time has been spent one-on-one with people sorting and sifting through their specific stories. It has been an amazing experience, and there really isn't anything I haven't seen or talked through with someone. I am not a therapist, I am not diagnosing or clinically helping people; I try to help people find that other side of the coin, the one that helps bring things into balance and gives them the chance to understand themselves better and to be ready to catch that wave of momentum that is coming their way. My work here is to get you into the best position in the lineup for that.

So, let's get to work now and create some momentum. Remember, there is no judgment here, just explorations, concepts, formulas, tools, etc., that I hope you will try out, get that sense of accomplishment from, and then get some healthy hope to keep you going down your path even further.

Stick with me. I've made so many mistakes—you might as well get a laugh or two, maybe see yourself in my craziness, and come away with some better plans made and the skills to follow through with them and make them stick.

Part I

ASSESS

Getting the Lay of the Land

It is time to get started. We gotta get all the puzzle pieces out on the table so we can get the lay of the land. See what you are working with, dealing with. How do we do that?

There are some key concepts and personal assessments we need to understand and carry out. And there is also a decision that needs to be made. Not so much a decision, but maybe a filter of sorts: to remain open-minded and receptive to the concepts in this book, even when they're abstract. I want this book to be full of practical advice that you can use to help your plans stick better. But I acknowledge that we are about to get into a lot about how our brains work, how our emotions influence our plans, and other deeper, "self-help"-feeling concepts. I wrestled with this, but ultimately, it is where we have to start. In all my work with people trying to make something of their lives, these things we will discuss are what get in the way most. They are mindsets and concepts that keep us from getting started on the road to making our plans a reality. So, I ask you to make a decision right here and now: Don't fight this part because it doesn't feel concrete or practical. Be fully open to it, knowing that any work you do on these mindsets and concepts will only help in making your plans stick while giving you the self-awareness to make sure that, once your plans start sticking, you can also maintain your momentum. My promise to you is to make all this as practical and real-world as possible.

Concept #1 or #1 Concept?

We are nothing more than a conglomeration of thoughts, feelings, and emotions we have either consciously or subconsciously decided to believe and act out, live, or hide behind. Soon, we will see how this adds up to patterns and how our brains can get tricky with those patterns and turn them for or against us, with things like cognitive distortions and other more negative mindsets.

That is the capital-T truth there.

Can you see it in your own life? Can you take a breath and reflect on the thoughts, feelings, and emotions that shape who you are and have led you to where you are now in life? Don't fear the result of asking yourself hard questions; just get the lay of the land. Be completely honest with yourself. It is all just data for later.

Our brains have to think tens of thousands of thoughts a day. These thoughts build up, or layer on top of each other, and begin to work for or against us until they subconsciously lead and guide who we are and the decisions we make. And for reasons that are within our control and out of our control, we decide at times to latch onto a few of those thoughts and make them our current truth. They tint our world, guide our decisions, and create peace or chaos.

Just think about it.

To a degree, I think we have all experienced a bit of bullying in this life—maybe from a playground tormentor in the third grade, or a parent who never had anything nice to say. It could have been a one-time experience or a repetitive experience that still wounds you today. Whether consciously or through no fault of our own, we took on those callous comments and wounding experiences and believed them fully; we put them in the driver's seat, and they became part of our story.

And they've been guiding and making decisions for us ever since, even though, more than likely, they aren't even close to our real truth. But those tens of thousands of thoughts race and mold and become more of our reality with each passing day.

In the introduction, we spoke about all those little ts and Big Ts that we all experience. They carry messages. Messages you believe to this day, and they are keeping you from staying motivated, believing in yourself, and carrying out your plans. You need to start to care about those messages, understand them, and listen to the stories they are telling you. This is where we start, now, in this moment. I don't want to start later with some better version of you; you can be completely stalled out or thriving, but these Ts and their messaging have laid the foundation for how you'll implement what's to come. If we don't acknowledge them, they stay in charge; if we do, well, the work begins to wrangle those messages and convert them into better ones, and to believe them.

This is a fancy way of saying:

Acknowledge/understand your messaging +

do the work creating healthier messaging =

new plans, routines, and habits =

a healthier, evolving version of you.

Analog Is Best

Full disclosure: I still use a calculator watch and prefer a film camera. I am old-school, not a hipster. I fantasize about owning a farm and playing tag with my kids, dogs, and some of those furry cows. I trust analog things more.

Early on in life, I realized that nothing made me more honest than a blank sheet of paper and a pen. There is something about staring at a blank white page. Anything goes. It feels both permanent and not. I also learned I could trust myself and my thoughts more as those ideas traveled from my brain, down my neck, through my arm, and ultimately moved the hand that moved the pen. It was therapeutic, honest, and real for me to face that blank canvas. I am going to ask you to do a lot of old-school, maybe quite analog exercises throughout this book, but here's the funny thing about us humans. Most of us reading will blow right by these exercises instead of pausing and letting the process play out. I am guilty too. I used to do this when reading a book with exercises. Please pause. Your brain is going to tempt you to keep reading; it wants something new and exciting instead of focusing on itself and changing. There will be a battle. Win that battle right here and now.

So, it is time to take a pause from my ranting and grab a journal, some paper, and a writing tool again. I am going to ask you some questions, and I need you to see this as an important moment to reflect and understand what stories are in your driver's seat. There is no judgment, just a desire to understand. But first a story to help me introduce a through line and some context.

Maui

A while back I was in Hawaii with a girl I was super into. We were having a great time, but at the same time, I wasn't getting or feeling any closer to her. I was devastated. I had such a good time, but I was dropping the ball again. I had had big hopes of really deepening our developing relationship in Hawaii, but I had failed. When I dropped her off at the airport in Maui, things just felt wonky; I felt almost dizzy, like I had been on a boat for a few days. I knew it was my same deal: I rush in, feel close, get scared, strangle the relationship with the worries I've had about a girl and me, watch the relationship crumble, get sad, travel somewhere else, and find a new crush. That was my cycle, and I was feeling it physically that day. It was the first time I felt like my patterns had sickened me. Maybe you've felt the same after you ruined another good plan of yours.

This time, when I got back to the house, I let myself sit in the mud of my situation. I just couldn't repeat the cycle anymore. It felt so familiar, yet so gross. I started asking myself questions, which we will do here now. It was hard, but it felt so good! I finally allowed myself to get the lay of my own land. I didn't have a journal, and there was no paper in the house, so I grabbed some toilet paper and started mapping out all the things I felt were getting in the way of me showing up better in the world.

Five Important Questions to Get You Started

1. Am I truly happy with my current situation? Freewrite and see what flows.

2. What am I not allowing myself to see about myself right now? Write, don't judge.

3. Have I had enough? Yes or no.

4. What do I know now that will make this time different? Explore what you know about yourself now that makes you ready.

5. Am I willing to fall off the horse, dust myself off, and ride again a few more times? Explore how committed you have been in the past and now.

These questions helped me get started. I didn't follow a guide; they just came intuitively. I let them. I think it came from that part of us that roots for and supports us—it really wanted me to know where I was really at. Yes, they are questions, but they felt like decisions at the same time.

Even after answering those questions, everything still felt pretty dammed-up. My creativity, my feelings, everything. I had been so stuck in my patterns for so long, I knew it was going to take a while to deconstruct it all. I had been ignoring myself for far too long by helping others and losing focus on myself. I didn't feel I was worth investing in. It should come as no surprise that a lot of my plans never worked when I was so lost in my patterns. Am I the only one who has felt that way? Based on my conversations with others, no.

Those initial questions greased the wheels and forced me to make some decisions. But I felt I needed to ask myself another deep question or two, to really get the ball rolling. I want you to ask these as well. Stop, ponder, and listen to yourself as you do.

Where am I feeling the most shame in my life? Why do I always feel so guilty? And what about?

So that's where I began, where we now begin—with where I was feeling the most shame, the most guilt in my life—as a way to start to understand why I chose to hold onto those experiences. I looked at my patterns with a bit more compassion after asking myself those questions. I could see these patterns almost trying to protect me from all that guilt and shame. Experiences from my youth had shaped me into a guilt-ridden, shame-filled people pleaser, yet my worn-out patterns created a strong leader and entrepreneur. A total contradiction.

That day in Hawaii, though, I wanted more. I wanted to get to the source of it all. I needed to change. And today, I need you to go through the same process. It won't be formulaic (what affects me may have no bearing on you), but the process will be the same for you.

What got mapped out on that long piece of toilet paper were experiences I had had that still guided me and my decisions to that very day. Because I asked myself those specific questions, apologies that I needed to make so I could clear some guilt became clear, experiences I wanted to have became important, and I found a bit of fun exploring who I still wanted to become. It took a hell of a lot of self-honesty. I didn't give up after five minutes. I stayed in the hard work until sunset.

As I walked to the beach to watch the sunset, I started feeling much lighter. That is what understanding does: it relieves us; it doesn't burden us. People had gathered to watch; I saw couples, old people, young people, and I just felt part of them. I wasn't feeling alone. I didn't envy the couples I saw. I just knew I had some work to do, and I made a commitment on that beautiful Maui evening to be in the driver's seat, not my past. To guard my thoughts, to watch my emotions, and not believe every feeling I had.

When I got home (and after a bomb sandwich and pudding from a local deli), I set some goals I knew would stick. I made some rough plans. Because of all of what I came to understand about myself, I knew I could follow through a bit better. I will talk about how to set better goals later, but I need you to know, I've accomplished them, all the goals I set that day. I wasn't born superhuman with the ability to just make things happen. I slogged it out. I fought and stayed in control. Why? Because I felt for once I had been truly honest with myself.

Courtesy of the author

This Works

You may notice that I am not citing research papers or quoting people. I do love reading and researching. I am not against it. What I am trying to do is to make this as accessible as possible, as real-world as I can. I didn't want to confuse the process I went through with the advice and case studies of others.

I have a little place in Mexico we lovingly call the beach shack. It has no electricity, no heated water, no internet, no fridge. We love being there. A long time ago, when I was going through this process, a friend and I spent a long weekend there. We surfed, ate, relaxed, and lay out in the sun talking about life. He was going through some similar things; his plans for himself just weren't working out. He had a great job and was progressing well, it seemed, but it didn't feel like his plans were really sticking well. He expressed that they didn't feel genuine to him. I hope you can relate to that. So, I opened up, which I rarely do, and shared what I was going through. It seems we were both stuck in different but similar ways. So, on one of our outings to get food, we also stopped by a local school supply store and bought some paper, some poster boards, some pens, and some knock-off Sharpies. I told him I was going to send him down the same path I'd gone down, and to see what he came up with. I wanted feedback on it. I wanted to know as well if this was working, or if I was crazy.

We started with the exact same questions I presented to you earlier. We started, as we all should, by chipping away slowly, trying to crack our vulnerability and old mindsets just a bit in the hopes we can see more clearly. Later that night, we built a fire, and we started on the following exercise.

Writing Exercise

We have unique stages in our lives:

- Childhood
- Elementary School
- Middle School
- High School
- College
- Job

And the list goes on.

I consider these stages or chapters or transitions—and you may have better/different names.

I feel that maybe most who are reading this have experienced a few of these stages, but you may feel there are other more important labels for yours. Don't get in the weeds too much.

Choose the ones you have experienced or are experiencing currently.

STAGES OF LIFE

1 Elementary School

- Forgetting to dress up for picture day, being messy
- Being left out by a neighbor
- Not having the right thing to eat on the field trip

2 Middle School

- Middle school dance nightmare, getting rejected
- Failing my first math test
- Not being able to keep up with clothing trends

3 High School

- Not knowing what I want to do after high school
- Failing my driver's license test four times!
- Having to always get rides because we couldn't afford a car for me

4 After Graduating

- Struggling at school with course load
- Not getting accepted by my favorite club
- A professor's really harsh critique of my paper, I worked so hard on it!

5 Close to now

- I feel totally unfulfilled at work
- My last break-up was awful, I never want to date again!
- I lost a parent to cancer

Write one down in the middle of a piece of paper and draw a box around it. Now we are going to sit and think about elementary school, let's say. Write down some good memories; sit with that time and see what comes up. Maybe you got a rad compliment from a teacher, or you felt those first butterflies in your stomach when you saw a classmate. Or maybe there are some heavier ones. I have some really Big Ts from this time period, but that's for another book. Don't shy away from painful memories. Sit in them, feel them; it makes them real and easier to heal.

Here's an example:

In third grade, I got rejected by Samantha. I thought she was so cute. I knew nothing about what to do except what those butterflies in my stomach told me to do. I needed to express my undying love for her. So, I went home and changed the lyrics to an old classic song, switched her name in, and sang it to her the next day at recess. I was quickly rejected.

It was my first rejection and it stung. I remember it clearly, so I knew it still had some power over me. I sat with that memory more; I felt it. How did it change me? What did I feel about myself as a result? I got rejected for the first time. It broke my invincibility. It hurt, and I also felt it also made me more afraid to express emotions outwardly.

A memory from third grade was clearly still having an effect!

I didn't know what to think when I was doing this exercise. I laughed a little bit. A bit at my naivety to think it was cool to sing a song to a girl in third grade, but also because it wasn't as traumatic an experience, looking back; it shouldn't be in the driver's seat still, or even in the back seat for that matter, but it was. I still felt it was unsafe to express my feelings or go out on a limb emotionally.

So, I wrote down "singing to Samantha" by the box labeled Elementary School. More memories, both positive and negative, came up: my first fight, being left out by friends... Each memory that surfaced and had weight to it, I put down.

What is this weight I am referring to? I simply believe it is a signal that other memories and meaning are attached to it, which means there's more exploring to be done. That is why we put it down: so we remember to dig around some more later.

Messaging = Mindsets

This is the process I want you to go through now. Just like I did. Be brave enough to sort through some of these stages in life and see what's contained in them. Get to know them, and try to decipher the messages they hold and what they've been telling you about yourself all this time. This is important work. As mentioned earlier, these messages combine to create who you are and how you see the world (your patterns), and then your brain and feelings take advantage of it all and play all sorts of tricks we will learn about.

Take as long as you need here. Take it in chunks, but please stick with it. If you remember it well, it is having an effect. Don't dismiss a memory of any experience. They don't all have to be negative, either. As you find those early positive memories, you'll more than likely see they became your strengths. But please, sit and experience it all again. Not to re-traumatize, but to understand the messages being carried. Then you can make some calls on it: is it really positive? more negative?

What message is the specific memory giving you?

Write that message out, clearly, in that box next to the memory.

We are trying to see all the messages swirling around; we want to become familiar with them, know them, and not ignore them any longer.

This is the key for our healing: to convert a heavy memory into a message. We can do something about a message.

Our familiarity with those messages will allow us in future chapters and in life to better label what we are feeling and change what is going on with us (our patterns). I repeat: This is important work.

So it was with me and my friend, and so it will be with you. We start with this exercise. We need, like I said, to get the lay of the land (all the messages). This is how we do it. Don't sell yourself short here. I am being bold when saying this exercise could change your life. I am not sending you through this exercise to give you excuses for why things are the way they are for you right now. We are doing this to unarrest our development. It is tempting to hide behind what we find out, and it might even feel a bit invalidating for me to even say that. Our Big Ts and little ts only have the power we give to them. We can't hide behind them or be too afraid to get to know them; that gives them infinite power. I am not minimizing their current power; I am just saying you are more powerful than they are. They don't want to arrest your development anymore; they think they are still protecting you. Honestly, from what I've learned through this process in my own life, they want you to learn so you can grow and ultimately teach others. Stick with me, please, and with yourselves.

As the fire died down that night, my friend and I had tons of papers all over the shack. It was, oddly, such a fun night—just laughing, and at times, silent. I noticed a tear or two from my friend, and I shed a few as well. We gathered all the papers up and were tempted to throw them in the fire. It is easy to just want to ignore it all again. We all have that pattern: make a big stride, then return to an easier pattern. It's the classic definition of self-sabotage.

But we now had real knowledge about our pasts and the messages we were holding onto. It was real.

My friend simply asked me, what's next?

Adult Perspective

Here's another story, and it was the next part of the journey I took my friend on. We went to bed that night and in the morning, we surfed, and I shared this story from when I was a little kid.

My grandpa picked me and my cousin up from my house in Los Angeles and drove us back to my grandparents' home for a sleepover.

We were super young. It's one of the stronger memories in my early childhood container. It has stuck with me a really good amount.

On the way to my grandparents' house, we stopped to drop something off at one of Grandpa's friends' homes. We waited outside the car. A kid approached us. I don't remember all the details; they are fuzzy. The kid was different. I was uncomfortable for some reason. He more than likely had some sort of handicap, and I wasn't nice. I can't pin the exact feelings I had or why I acted like I did. I had a cousin with disability, and I'd been his protector and greatest ally. I don't know really what happened, but I do remember that my grandfather was stern and very cross with me for my actions with that kid. The memory is very negative for me. The guilt and the shame of it all were super strong.

The message I was getting from that experience: I am a total jerk, a bad person. I could use harsher words (I do in my mind). I imagine you probably have used some harsh words toward yourself because of some of your memories.

For some reason, I didn't show up well with a kid who really didn't deserve whatever it was that I did. My grandpa noticed, and he made me understand that day that my actions were not right. It was a powerful experience with a lasting message.

When that memory came up in Maui, I realized I have gone out of my way to be nice and accommodating since that day. I realized I hated that I had showed up in a way that not only made my grandfather disappointed in me, but probably caused that kid some hurt feelings as well. As I sat in that memory, I could still feel its power. It was heavy.

You may find some memories like this as you go through each stage in your life—moments we aren't proud of. I told my friend the story, and of course, he made fun of me. How could I be holding onto that? I was so young! I didn't even remember what I said or did. But he also understood; he had a similar memory.

He shared with me a rough story. He'd come home from school proud that he'd gotten a decent grade on an assignment he'd really struggled with. It wasn't close to an A, but it was a battle he survived and won. His dad, instead of noticing the battle wounds and the pride in my friend's eyes, tore him a new one because he hadn't gotten an A. My friend never went to college. He stayed in the trades. He realized he had lost his steam around academics on that day, and that other memories had collected to tell him he wasn't a good student. I told him about my math teacher who told me to give up my dream of being an architect because I was lousy at math, so I did, and that one still stings because I am still head over heels for design and architecture.

We are all okay. Bringing this stuff up is tough. Don't spin out. You are okay. My friend and I just lay out under the sun, totally bummed that we had given up on parts of our plans because of these memories and messages. There is hope and a formula to practice that got us back on track.

You see, I am not who I was when I treated that kid that way back in the day, but in Maui and in Mexico, it seemed like a lot of these memories were piling up and I needed a way to heal them and move on from them. It was getting overwhelming.

*Side note before we begin: This process works whether the memory is from your childhood, or it happened two weeks ago. Hurt and struggle can be created in an instant and quickly attach to other, more distant memories and messages. We are focused on the weight of memory, no matter when it occurred. You got this (!!!) even if you made a significant blunder yesterday, or last month. Ground yourself in your present self and perspective as you go through this process.

Here is the best way I did it. It is simple yet powerful. It is the simple act of breathing our adult perspective onto a memory. What? Let me explain.

As I sat with that memory, I began to realize I was young, really young. Adult me said I really didn't know what I was doing, and that I can't judge who I am now because of something I did when I was younger. I was still learning about love, life, and compassion. And I had apologized to the kid, I had learned from it, I had felt all the things I needed to feel for the lesson to be complete. The inner adult telling me all this made me feel better. I gained some clarity and saw things a little differently.

If you are young and reading this and don't quite feel you have the right perspective on a particular memory, you can seek a trusted person in your life to help you see it from a kinder, more mature perspective. Or ask yourself: *What would future, adult me tell me about how I should be thinking about this memory and its message?*

I had my friend do the same thing. We were finding the other side of the coin to the messages we had held onto for so long. We sat there looking at the waves in silence, but I knew in our heads we were trying to find an adult perspective or alternate/mature message to these weighty memories. It was like we were rehearsing them in our minds until we believed them. The new messages were true, but it took some time to convince our brains that the old messaging was false and worn out. Every time that memory—or the feeling around that memory—comes up, I show it the other side of the coin, I give it some adult perspective.

As we packed up the towels and grabbed our boards, my friend said to me, "Maybe I will go get trained as a paramedic."

And I said, "Maybe I am not such a jerk, after all."

You aren't the messages you've been believing for quite some time now, either.

Evidence-Based Thinking

In this process of changing messaging, I knew I needed to go a little further. Our brains can get us back to our old messaging and patterns quickly.

Did the evidence of my life since then support the message that I am a total jerk and worthless? Did my friend have piles of evidence telling him he couldn't succeed in an academic environment? Do you have stacks of evidence proving your worn-out messaging?

Evidence-based thinking is one of the greatest tools in our toolbox. If we can be honest with ourselves and stick with ourselves in the mud, we can begin to gather evidence that either supports or completely dismantles the messages we believe about ourselves.

I was realizing how much that experience with my grandpa had shaped who I was by the fact that it held such strong negative feelings and that I built a life helping others and putting myself last. So, I started to gather evidence to support those strong feelings. I looked in all my containers. High school, middle school, college, and beyond. I never repeated the incident. I couldn't find a single piece of evidence that says, "Hey Josh, you have a pattern of treating people who are different from you negatively or unfairly." So, I wrote next to the old messaging and the adult perspective (the new messaging) all the evidence I had gathered to prove the true and new messaging I was trying to assimilate.

> Another side note here: the evidence could have come back and said: "Hey, you know what Josh, there is a pattern here, a not-so-good one. I think it merits a deeper look and some change." That is okay too, because I used an adult perspective and evidence-based thinking to arrive at my *current* truth and that is a reality from which I can work, it is my present-day truth. So, then what? We set a new vision for ourselves (like those initial thoughts we wrote down at the beginning of this book), we plan, and then we get to work (doing what we will learn from here on out).

> A side note to the other side notes: In Create and Do, the stories fall off a bit as we get into the nitty-gritty of skills, tools, and exercises to practice. In these sections, you are beginning to formulate and practice new stories for yourself. Please take the inspiration from my

stories and let them guide and propel you into creating and practicing new and healthier stories.

Back to My Friend and Me at the Beach Shack

I had my friend do that over lunch at the beach shack. Please do that now for yourself. List all the evidence you can to back up your new messaging.

From this adult or more mature perspective, I could see what was true and what was false more readily. You will too. I could see those negative feelings about myself just weren't true. So, I could let them go. The evidence against it was too strong.

The evidence gives us permission to let go or change.

If they rise up again, and they still do, I recite the new messaging and all the evidence, and they still go away quickly. It has been years since I have felt those strong feelings. The evidence is just too strong for me to believe that those negative emotions are true, because they aren't, and I didn't want to live out that old messaging any longer.

Adult perspective + evidence-based thinking = the best truth we have.

Many a spiritual leader has said in one way or another that the truth will set us free, or in other words, it will heal the memory, counteract its negative messaging, and heal us.

Memorize that formula. Live from truth, always. Your brain will for sure try over and over to bring you back to the old messaging and we will get into that here soon, but the evidence should quash your brain's attempt to try to gain that power back.

This Takes Time

I mentioned that I had a cousin who was disabled both mentally and physically. He was a stud of a young man who unfortunately passed early from brain cancer. I still had a lot to learn from him.

There were many times growing up when he and I would play basketball for hours, ride our bikes, or wash and rewash the family cars. I didn't always mind it, but at times, it could feel like a lot. Because of his disability, he could be intense and a handful. At times I wished for a break—I am naturally an introvert; my social battery is weaker than most.

When I was burning out on playing with my cousin, those feelings of guilt and shame from way back then with my grandpa would be screaming at me. That experience with that unknown kid all those years ago would guilt-trip me into sticking it out with my cousin and going well beyond burnout. I wish now that I'd had then a crude version of these skills I am teaching you in this book; it would have saved me years of building a personality that burned itself out helping others. Instead of taking care of myself a bit, I was constantly feeling bad, anxious that I wasn't being a good cousin or person. So many different emotions, all that tired and negative messaging about who I was as a person. I remember one time when I was about fourteen, I'd been playing basketball and just needed a break. I started feeling guilty. I looked for a way out, or a way to justify how I was feeling. Once again, the message was: you are a bad person for wanting to take a break or needing some time to yourself. I ended up in the bathroom crying because I couldn't handle it all.

I wish I had breathed some adult perspective and had the evidence I have now telling me I needed to see this situation differently. When I was with my cousin, it wasn't about me or him; it was about connecting and sharing time, and that was great, but burning myself out trying to soothe the old messaging that I was a jerk and a bad person wasn't so great.

Remember, the evidence can soothe and point out things we need to change if we are open to it. Sometimes, the evidence will be overwhelmingly in favor of your feelings of anxiety or guilt, but that evidence is just pointing you to something you need to work on and change. Trust the evidence but keep it positive. Let it soothe you, but also let it guide you toward your best self and the new messaging and plans you want to create.

If I had gathered evidence over the years that, in fact, I was a total jerk, well, then I would have had some things to work on and change. Remember, the evidence in my case said that I wasn't a jerk, but I needed to take care of myself more and help people for reasons other than guilt and shame.

I am trying to live that new message now.

Rehash

Adult perspective finally lets you see things from another angle.

The evidence soothes and then guides you toward your next steps.

Trust that formula.

My buddy now is a paramedic and changing lives. He aced his schooling. He created new messaging, left behind being a victim to the old messaging, and used his life experience to breathe adult perspective on his new plans. He didn't see the old messaging the way he had before; he saw promise and opportunity and a chance to deliberately practice. He really changed that weekend. There was hope all over the place. The evidence was just too overwhelming that he and I could both do things differently if we just practiced that formula.

We Have Begun to Map the Memories of Your Mind

You may have noticed in your life that it has been extremely difficult to stay consistent or follow through with plans you have made. Maybe you've started a college semester, got overwhelmed, and impulsively dropped all your classes. Or it is possible you started a job and, after a few shifts, found something you didn't like about it and then quit. It is also possible you are totally stuck in your room, avoiding life completely.

By finding these memories and their messages to you, you are in fact beginning to own your story, as it is now, without gloss or glitter. Owning our story makes it real. Making plans, which we will learn to do in coming sections, will stick if we are real with ourselves. If we know the map of our mind, the excuses it will make, the memories that will come surging, and the feelings that will overwhelm us once we've decided to do something new or different, then we've set ourselves up so much better to fight another round.

I hope you will take the exercises I set out seriously. Your memories are messages, and you need to be familiar with those messages. Then you need to take that breath and start to see them anew, from a more mature and kind perspective, and then find the evidence to back that new perspective up. And as I said, if the evidence clearly says something needs to change, well, this is the perfect book to help you make plans around those needed changes.

Recap

1. Blank sheet of paper.

2. Write out all the stages of life you've lived thus far.

3. Label them, box them, give them a container with room to breathe.

4. Let the memories surge, all of them, both positive and negative.

5. Write them around the box (if they are heavy, make sure they are written down).

6. What messages did you take from those memories?

7. Write those messages down clearly, feel them, and make sure they ring true.

8. Find the other side of the coin and breathe some adult perspective onto the messages.

9. What is true about those memories and messaging? How does your adult mind and experience feel you should see them now?

10. What does the evidence of your life say about those memories and messaging? True? Blown out of proportion? Totally false?

11. Let the evidence both soothe and guide.

12. Repeat the process and the formula over and over.

13. Any time your brain wants to go back to the old messaging, show it the evidence.

14. Believe yourself.

I knew I wasn't crazy when I saw the process work with my friend. He told me he loved it because it really was simple, and he could memorize that formula. But mostly, he was relieved: he had evidence to back up his new plans and he could finally put to rest the old and tired messaging.

Adding Up the Dopamine

I am no scientist or researcher, but I am curious. I hope you will be as well on this journey. You've begun to understand your memories and their messages to you. I want to dive into validation/dopamine. I am creating this discussion from my observations and gut feelings.

Dopamine—a chemical your body releases; it is pleasurable, positive.

Validation—a need we all have; we want to know we exist, so we seek validation.

While dopamine and validation are not the same, they are interconnected in the brain's reward system. When we receive validation from others, whether through praise, acknowledgment, or acceptance, it can trigger the release of dopamine, contributing to feelings of pleasure and satisfaction.

Put more simply, dopamine hits are mostly positive, and we seek more dopamine as much as we can. Dopamine validates our existence; it rewards our actions and, to me, it validates who we are and who we are becoming.

I need you to go through another exercise.

Dopamine (+) Addition (+)

I need us to add up the dopamine and find out what it says about us, and then we need to decide if we want to be that sum of all our dopamine hits.

Let me explain.

I was getting frustrated on a call with a young man I was coaching. Try as we might, we weren't getting any traction. I knew what was going on, but he didn't want to see it. I saw a young man paralyzed by a fear of failure in his post-college career. He saw his previous bosses and co-workers as people trying to stifle his creativity and style. He was unemployed and playing video games all day.

So, I took him through this exercise. I had him start adding up where he got all his dopamine hits from. He made me a list. Gaming (of course), food, weed, being on Discord with friends, girls, sex, the sports bar with friends—there were a few more I can't recall well. I simply asked him to sum up what type of person is created by all these dopamine hits. The conversation was enlightening for him.

After some thought, he summed it quite succinctly: "I'm a lonely gamer." I asked him if that was what he wanted or had envisioned for himself. It wasn't. So, I asked him, "If you had a blank sheet of paper, where would you want to get your dopamine from?"

He rattled off another list for me: being creative, riding the subway to a job, drinks with friends, better exercise habits, different hobbies—the list went on.

I told him it seemed like he knew exactly the priorities and plans he wanted to put into place for himself. He agreed. But there were still things getting in his way.

Why does this matter?

It is not often that we can get a view so simply and succinctly of who we are. Fast, too. Add up your dopamine hits: that is who you are. That is what you go after, strive for, and are becoming.

Do you like that person? Don't judge. Yes or no?

Dopamine is just evidence. It will point you to your work.

Time to Really Start Assessing

Reminder: I swear to you that this is a book on making your plans stick. They already are, I promise. Stick with me. I would hate to just send you down a list of goal setting, habit building, and starting routines. They wouldn't stand a chance. Your brain and mindsets are too powerful.

We will begin now to dive into concepts, attitudes, and ideas that I need you to assess for you to truly understand what is getting in the way of following through with your plans. But I need to first wrap up this dopamine discussion.

Why We Can't Change

This lonely gamer couldn't find traction because he was getting his dopamine validation from other, more compelling activities, not necessarily positive, that provided his brain with little incentive to change. This realization highlights a fundamental aspect of our behavior.

Dopamine plays a key role in the brain's reward and pleasure centers. It helps motivate our actions by providing a "feel-good" reward when we engage in activities we enjoy or achieve something. However, if someone frequently engages in activities that release dopamine, they might find less motivation to pursue new or challenging endeavors because the existing activities already satisfy their brain's reward system.

Additionally, our memories, particularly those linked with emotions, can reinforce our current behaviors. If our experiences are positive and tied to certain activities, they contribute to a cycle where we continue engaging in these activities, further increasing dopamine release and reinforcing the behavior.

This dynamic is crucial to understanding why changing habits or mindsets can be challenging.

The "feel-good" state is like a baseline—a place where you are comfortable, a state that your brain strives to maintain. Your brain needs this stability, craves it, and will resist changes that threaten it.

This is how our mindsets are created.

If you game for eight hours a day and you like it and you do it often enough, it soon becomes your baseline, your brain acclimates, and then it will fight bravely to maintain that baseline.

We all deal with this. We all have our own baseline. By mapping out memories and their messages, by understanding the sum of your dopamine, you are beginning to understand your personal baseline.

Doing these exercises may get you down. Totally natural. They are raw and honest conversations. Things haven't been working out for us because we didn't have the right evidence and adult perspective, we weren't playing with a full deck.

I can't wait to jump into the next steps, but I wanted to give you a hit of dopamine now, in the form of hope, in the form of neuroplasticity.

I'll stop saying this, I swear, but I am no scientist. I am not going to get the particulars around neuroplasticity down in the best way. Doesn't matter, I can sum it up, and tell you the hope it gave me when I learned about it.

Neuroplasticity basically is the fact that the brain can rewire, or reorganize, and be different from what it was before, at any age really, with effort and understanding. I don't have to be who I was yesterday, and that was the greatest revelation science has made, for me personally, in a long time! I can change, and I have the science to prove it. Neuroplasticity is healing evidence; it soothed me deeply. I hope it does the same for you. You can change. You can rewire your brain. Your baseline can become what you want it to be; you can get your dopamine from healthy and positive sources. It is all possible with effort. The brain won't rewire by itself; you gotta give it better dopamine validation, better priorities, goals, habits, hobbies, and messages, along with an adult perspective and all the right evidence. Only then will things start to improve—rapidly. This process will become routine and welcomed.

Back from Maui Now

I learned this when I got back from Maui. I set some big plans for myself there, especially around my relationships. Remember, I was failing hard in the relationship department. I needed a bridge, a place where I could learn and grow, which we will get into later. I was thirty-four at the time, and there were some things happening around me that needed some attention and clear action.

One of those decisions was about two boys in an orphanage in Mexico who I felt strongly connected to. Things were happening there that were out of their control, but I saw I could have a bigger role in their lives, so I started building a bridge in my mind.

Before I dive further into that story and other examples, I need to introduce some concepts and ideas to you that are like seeds I want to plant. You will need to assess where you are at with each one of these concepts and ideas. I will give you some things to think about, questions to ask yourself, with the hope that they will be present when you make your new plans, because, as you will see, these things will for sure get in the way of you following through.

Are you ready to assess more and dive in deeper? The next section blew my mind.

Cognitive Distortions

When I first learned about cognitive distortions, I laughed a whole lot. I thought to myself, "Why am I just learning about these things at age thirty-five?" It seemed like a conspiracy: let's not teach anyone about these things that have such a grip on our lives and brains.

Simply defined, cognitive distortion is a mental filter through which you see life. Cognitive distortions are usually not positive; they work in the background, and we often don't know they are in control of how we view life and then act.

Everyone has them. If you don't think you do, you are lying to yourself. We have our favorite ones, and you need to get to know yours so you can catch them quickly when they take charge. If you do that, I can't describe to you how good you will feel. Very empowering indeed.

Here are some quick examples of the top cognitive distortions out there. Use the ole internet and go down a rabbit hole on this topic; it is worth it. You'll see yourself in a few of the most common cognitive distortions. My hope here is that, by bringing these to the top of your mind, they'll stick there, and you can make different choices on how to think about things because you have this knowledge. That is how this works. Knowledge truly is power.

Try these on for size:

Black-and-White Thinking

It is either this way or that way. No gray. This cognitive distortion is sometimes called all-or-nothing thinking; it is based in rigidity, maybe even stubbornness. When seeing life through this filter, you can only see your point of view or current feelings. New ideas can't be seen well. New perspectives are shunned. It is either one way or the other. When we are trapped in this cognitive filter, we can't get creative, we can't begin anew, with nearly anything. We fight battles, give up, or don't engage because our options for seeing the world are limited and rigid.

Real-World Example

Imagine being stuck having to be perfect at everything you do or being a complete failure at everything all the time. No in-between. Perfection or failure. That is black-and-white thinking, that rigidity against practicing or trying anything new because you are either going to hit home runs every time or strike out, a solid base hit is never an option. When our mind gets this way, our emotions also seem to swing to those extremes as well.

Catastrophizing

Here's a fun one. This filter paints everything as a disaster. My friend hasn't called me back in an hour, they're mad at me, or maybe worse! Our brain takes information and turns it into the worst-case scenario. Our anxiety skyrockets, our emotions rise, we get flushed and blinded to reality: the world could literally be coming to an end because you chose the wrong emoji at the end of your last text to the person you are crushing on.

Real-World Example

I feel we all know this distortion very well. It is a knee-jerk reaction.

I get a D+ on an exam. This leads to, "I am a horrible student, I won't amount to anything, I should just drop out of school altogether." Once this snowball gets going, it leads toward nothing but the worst-case scenario, a total catastrophe.

Or, before you even attempt something, you decide it is already a complete disaster, or imagine the worst-case scenario will come to be. In the same sentence you say, you are madly in love with a person, but they will never fall for you because in your mind you are the worst person in the world, and they'll see it right away. Your brain stops you again from having any options because the worst of the worst will always happen. Why try?

Future-Tripping

It has been said that our minds are typically either in the past or in the future, rarely in the present moment. This filter keeps us out of the present. It's a bit of a funky cognitive distortion because I believe it uses our past experiences to totally trip out about the future, thereby forcing us to relinquish our control over the present. *What if this happens? What if that happens?* It also looks like you or me sitting, daydreaming, fantasizing about some possible event or scenario in the future. At times, we can get sucked into future-tripping by dreaming about some cool upcoming experience until our fears and other cognitive distortions creep in and turn things toward the negative. You know are future-tripping if you spend most of your time thinking about the future, as dictated by your past.

Real-World Example

My mind loves this one.

Let's go on vacation to Hawaii! Awesome! Wait, what about the plane ride? How will traffic be on the way to the airport? Will my sunscreen ruin the reefs? Will my relationship last until then? Things turn negative quickly and, all of a sudden, this nice trip becomes overwhelming to plan, not worth it, and totally anxiety-ridden. Hawaii doesn't happen.

Mind Reading

This one is hard for me. I struggled with it for a long while. My experiences with Supergirl and other relationships turned me into quite the mind reader. I knew the relationship was over because I knew from a look or a comment what the other person was "truly" thinking. I would doom any type of relationship growth because I could read minds and I knew what someone felt about me, and it was rarely good. You can't read minds; you can only communicate, look for evidence, and communicate some more. Mind reading stops your growth. It is nothing more than your fears projected onto another.

Real-World Example

Your one true love is in front of you. The conversation is going great. *But wait, they didn't laugh hard enough at my joke. They looked away. Maybe they don't like me. Maybe I'm seeing this all wrong. They probably hate my shirt. My one crooked tooth is becoming the deal-breaker. I know it! This is over. Ask them how they feel? Why? I can read it all over their face. I am not good enough. I will never be. Time to give up.*

Discounting the Positive

This cognitive distortion loves the word "but." I just got a B+ on my biology exam, but...fill in the next part with something negative that discounts the positive. Our brains are weird. We shy away from celebrating success. The brain is so concerned about maintaining its baseline that it will even discount the positive things going on in our lives. Why? **Because it is less vulnerable.**

It is easier to explain away a failure than to maintain a bunch of wins.

It takes more effort to smile than frown, more effort to succeed than fail, and your brain knows it. This cognitive distortion, I believe, will sneakily ruin all your plans. Watch out for it!

Real-World Example

This one also has "should" all over it. That is the most real-world example I can give. If you are using the word "should" in most of your inner conversations, then you are probably discounting the positive. "Should" means you are focusing on some way to be better or do better. It is not always a bad thing, but take note: are you quickly going negative when there's something good or even neutral going on?

I got a B. I should have gotten an A.

They finally called me, but they should have called me earlier.

I finished my workout, but I should have done a few more reps.

Build on your positive momentum; don't "should" on it.

More Where These Came From

These are just five in a long list of cognitive distortions that our mind uses to create filters for how we see the world. Get to know yours. Look for examples of how they show up in your life. That understanding will stick in your self-awareness. You'll notice when you are stuck in one of them quicker and quicker and you'll be aware and ready to do something different.

That is how change works.

Change Formula

This is an important formula for life. My formulas might seem weird or oddly written. Remember, they are steps you can take and repeat that truly create a specific outcome.

Learn something new about yourself +

make sure you understand it well +

stick it in your self-awareness +

you'll notice quicker when it shows up +

you'll be at a choice point +

you can then choose to do something more positive for yourself or different =

you begin to change

Before I learned about cognitive distortions, I simply thought I was unable to change some of my behaviors. Learning about how my mind took a rough and incredibly sad experience in my life, like Supergirl, and made me always catastrophize and mind read was empowering. Those cognitive distortions didn't allow me to trust myself, to learn the lesson well, and therefore to change. They kept me stuck, stagnant. Plans failed all around me.

I see quickly now when I am in one of those filters, and I hope you will too.

You can change. Get to know your pet cognitive distortions immediately.

Courtesy of the author

Failure

This is a rough assessment. It is never easy to sit in your failures. We all have them, the scars and somewhat fresh wounds of a time when we couldn't quite make it happen. Luckily, you aren't alone in this. We need to understand what failures you are holding onto. We need to get specific and, as we learned previously with our trip down Memory Lane, each one of these failures carries a specific message you and I have chosen to believe. There is a lot of hope in failure, because there is learning there and a way forward, if you choose. At times we button up our failures with tidy messages like, "Well, looks like I'll never be successful," or with an idea like, "I'll never put myself out there again because that last relationship was a total disaster." Like I did when I was failing at math and gave up my dream of architecture.

Failure doesn't have to be so neat and tidy. It isn't black and white. You need to know and believe that when one door closes, another one truly does open. You just might not see it because you wanted it to look like something else, or you rushed to clean up the mess and move on quickly. Don't. Sit with it so you can learn.

Failing All Around Africa

I traveled to South Africa and what was then Swaziland in 2007. It was an exploratory trip. That Mexico trip I took at the beginning of this book had turned rapidly into a successful and thriving not-for-profit. We were looking for more projects to support. We had put a lot of effort in. People wanted to be a part of what we were doing. We were also making mistakes left and right, learning daily.

So, we partnered up with another nonprofit and shared time, resources, and expertise crisscrossing southern Africa, looking for a project we could all believe in.

Africa is a gem. Each country has its own beautiful rhythm and culture. I had lived in Morocco for about eight months in 2000, and it felt so great being back on the continent. I was excited to bring a project home that my staff and board could discuss and then support.

But we were striking out left and right. You get good at sniffing out good projects. You learn what to look for and what questions to ask. You can sniff out a project with no heart or values quickly. You can also get sick of the show after a while.

One day, we came upon a project in Swaziland that seemed promising. It supported and educated child-headed households in the local area. At the time, HIV was ravaging Swaziland. You literally saw no one in their thirties. Just kids and their grandparents. A lot of these kids were raising their brothers and sisters on their own and with the support of the local community and projects like the one we were visiting.

We showed up one day and visited with the project's executive director. She was cordial, yet a bit aloof. A short time into our meeting, I finally understood why. We were one of many American nonprofits that had stopped by over the years. Always, tons of promises were made, not a lot of follow-through. Americans can at times barrel into a country with ideas for change and growth that don't really align with the local needs or culture. She had seen it all many times before.

She let us know her feelings, and I was instantly on the defense. I was twenty-six, I knew everything! I knew how to help! I had a successful thing going on, and a fresh college degree in advertising. How could she not see I was her guy! My ego was screaming. We were polite, so was she; she gave us a tour of the project and I wanted in. Badly. It was perfect, but ultimately my help, support, and guidance was not needed. We said our goodbyes; I was sort of sad-pissed. I wasn't getting what I wanted, and I was licking my ego's wounds.

That trip ended with no solid path forward for Kaiizen in Swaziland or South Africa. On the flight home, I was trying to come up with what to say to everyone. I had spent close to three weeks in southern Africa with nothing to show. I had failed.

Months went by, and I couldn't shake what I saw at that small but powerful project in Swaziland. It had amazing kids, an organized and loving staff, and real, measurable goals and programs. I got sad-pissed every time I thought about it, and those feelings of failure opened fresh wounds again and again. I was super busy after that trip, but was still wallowing in a way. We had plenty of trips to Mexico planned, and Brazil even, but my experiences in Morocco at a refugee camp for Western African immigrants had had a huge impact on my life and I wanted to help again on the continent. In many ways, I was wanting to make up for failures I still carried from my time at that refugee camp.

Maybe you have felt the same; totally stuck in your failures, with no way out. I was there, and even though I was seeing a lot of success in other areas, that failed exploratory trip ripped me up because of some previous experiences of failure in Africa. They, like those memories and messages we spoke of earlier, were starting to compound. Soon, one failed exploratory trip felt a lot heavier by the day. Memories and messaging stack and stack on top of each other.

I came to learn later that little brilliant flashes of inspiration still come while we are wallowing in our failures. They came to me as passing thoughts like, *Why don't you go back and prove your heart to that woman?* Or I would get into a fantasy about flying there with a big check in hand and proving to my ego, not her, that I was worth my salt in the industry. This went on for months. Finally, one of those thoughts I promise we all get flashed into my mind: *just do something about it* was what I felt. So, I found the courage to do something.

I have come to learn to trust this process deeply. Often, we don't because we are stuck and blind to what is showing up in our lives.

There are opportunities to be seen. There truly are.

There are chances to be had again. They are subtle. Like a little burst of momentum hoping to be felt and grasped onto. Or just a little thought like the one I had, a little whisper of hope and momentum: "Josh, why don't you just do something?" A message so simple can often be enough to start seeing things differently.

Have you noticed this too?

Have you found paths post-failure that were surprising and ultimately just as cool and satisfying? They will come as we breathe more adult perspective into our current situations and gather evidence. It is nothing more than breathing room to see these little inspirations.

So, what did I do with that little thought: *just do something*?

I convinced two dear friends to come with me to Swaziland again. I had no real plans. I simply promised them I would show them a good time and that my only goal was to win this lady over. Luckily, I have some amazingly supportive friends who are down for any adventure.

Almost serendipitously, when we arrived back at the project property in Swaziland almost a year post-rejection, the executive director was driving away in her car. I waved her down and we talked through our windows.

"Do you remember me?"

She was floored; she did, and she told us to come back at a specified time. She drove away in shock.

We ran to the store before our meet-up. We filled our tiniest of rental cars to the brim with food supplies, hygiene items, and the like. I could barely get my friend in the back seat, let alone get the car to move. We showed up at our meeting, unloaded the supplies, and that lady has now become one of my greatest mentors to this day.

I am so glad I didn't give up. So much goodness followed me not giving up. Some of the proudest and most impactful moments of my life came after that meeting, on the rich red soil of Swaziland. That little flash of momentum has led to Kaiizen affecting tens of thousands of lives monthly.

I am no one special. There are plans for you to be made and we will get you there. We just need to accept the failures we have made, learn from them, then wait for the next bit of inspiration to guide us toward our next steps. They will come if you are open and not wallowing like I was. They'll come if you are wallowing like me too.

Remember, you wrote a few big hopes and dreams at the beginning of this book. Those are 100 percent possible.

Failure Formula

I came up with this formula to help guide me through my failures:

Feel it +

don't personalize it + (don't get offended by it)

set the lesson(s) +

wait for the next steps/inspirations =

embrace another chance.

Let me make sense of that. Failure is inevitable. Instead of running from it, as they say in business, fail hard and fast. Feel the failure, don't avoid those feelings or push them away. But make sure you don't personalize. This is the hardest part. The lesson from every failure can't be *I am a worthless turd*. That is personalizing (a cognitive distortion). You can't find the lesson or the insight if you personalize all of it; you'll just wallow and get even more stuck if you do.

In a weird way, you need to seek out the lesson(s) from your failures. You must proactively take stock before the self-loathing and the self-pity come knocking. The faster you take these steps, the quicker you will fail and find a better way of doing it all. If you seek and accept the lesson, then you can be patient with yourself until the next idea or step becomes clear, and then you will feel some more hope because you get another chance.

Action Items from This Section

I want to help you live the above formula, so grab another sheet of paper.

1.   List your failures, the ones you are still holding onto.
     It's all okay.

2.   Get to know your feelings of failure. Feel them. Everyone feels
     them differently.

3. Resolve every message that comes up that doesn't help you create momentum. This is a great time for you to use the earlier formula of: **breathe adult perspective + find the evidence = best truth you have currently.**

4. This process will stop you from personalizing.

5. Next to the list of your failures, write down some lessons learned and play out the importance of those lessons in your mind. Find memories and examples that allow you to see how those lessons have served you. This helps set the lessons in stone.

6. Then you wait. You keep staying positive, grounding yourself in the lessons, and waiting for the next opportunity.

You will get another chance.

Hyper-Novelty

Dopamine seeking is the enabler of our society's hyper-novel nature. Slowly, you've been conditioned to want more, seek more, need more, from any given moment of the day. This becomes unsustainable; you easily become addicted to newness, and that newness can come in a variety of forms. Scrolling, substances, gaming, shopping—you name it, once you get the dopamine hit and you like it, the initial stoke will die down, and you'll need more; you'll need newness.

Sit with this for a moment and play out some hyper-novel moments in your life.

Learning to reflect this way is important.

Sitting down. Putting your phone far away. Eliminating distractions. Imagining in your mind how things are from an outside perspective.

I call this "getting the 10,000-foot view," as if you were in an airplane looking down at what is real in your life.

Can you see your hyper-novelty from this outside perspective, this 10,000-foot view?

Does it feel in check, or do you feel an incessant need for stimulation and newness?

What other questions would you want to ask yourself while you are in 10,000-foot view?

I've done this same exercise many a time. Watching myself scroll endlessly on a social media platform, antsy, feeling bored. Or numbing out watching a show because I am bored and locked in an old pattern. We all do it. Our culture seeks the novel and the new, almost incessantly now, and that brings you to a choice point that will influence who you will become far into the future. As we progress in this book, we will focus on your priorities and hobbies. Do you want to continue feeding this hyper-novel person inside of you?

Could this be an issue with time management and your relationship with boredom?

We need to assess this as we make plans for your future. Why?

Your long-term plans are at stake. How?

Plans take time. They aren't always exciting. Goals take time to achieve, and routines are established by hard-won consistency.

Here are some interesting questions: Where does your boredom take you now? What could you do with the time spent shopping online, or seeking other unhealthy dopamine hits that you hope will last just a little bit longer than the last one did? Who could you become with a solid investment in some true and lasting curiosity? Or with better management of your time? Would you play an instrument? Learn a craft? Anything?

Unfortunately, we end up living between two extremes: one a sort of manic hyper-novel state, the other being totally lazy and not willing to engage in life.

Your time is worth so much more.

Assessing Time Management

Sunday	Monday	Tuesday	Wednesday	Thursday	Friday	Saturday
Woke up	Looked for a Job	Couldn't sleep	5 jobs apps in	nothing	Job follow up	Clean a little
On the phone	Walked Dog	Hard day!	Video games		Looked at jobs	Drove around
Saw Mikey	Ate	Friends at work			Resume review	Looked for jobs
Ate		Fight w/ parents			Walked dog	
More Phone		lazy day			bored	
					bored	
					bored	

Yes, grab a piece of paper. I won't apologize this time. Remember, analog is best in this process.

Write: Sun (space) Mon (space) Tues (space), all the way to Saturday, across the top of the page. Probably best if the paper is horizontal for this one.

Think of last week. Under each day (basically a column), write what you did on each day.

1.   If you can't remember well, it signals that you were probably caught up in a lot of in-the-moment dopamine-seeking.

2.   What patterns do you see? Did you invest in meaningful things? Was it all random? Did you do anything consistently?

3.   Did you enjoy what you did? Put a star by what brought you joy or meaning.

4.   Look on your phone or take a guess, how much time did you spend online during the week, per day?

5.   Last step, a simple equation: put down below, for each day, how many hours you felt engaged.

Example:

    Online (from your phone notifications): 5.5 hours daily

    Engaged: 1.25 hours daily

    No shame or guilt. Remember, we are assessing. This is data. We need to see this data. We need to see how we are investing our time. If we don't like it, then we will just make better plans from here on out.

Laziness

The hard part of laziness is that it feels so good. Just like every other concept in this section, you need to become very familiar with your personal version of laziness.

Simple Josh Formula

Laziness = perfecting the art of excuse-making

We are lazy for a lot of reasons.

1. Fear of failure

2. Lack of drive

3. Lack of creativity

4. Confidence

5. Messaging from our past

    And lastly, because it can mask itself as something positive very, very easily. Trust me, I know. That formula is key. If you are being lazy, you need to ask yourself: What excuses am I making for myself?

    I mean it.

    Write those excuses down. Make that list.

    Sample list from my life:

1. I'll put off exercise because I have worked a long day and I deserve a break.

2. I won't call this person because it feels like conflict, which feels like work.

3. Instead of engaging in this hard work project, I'll go help this person.

Get familiar with yours. Plant them, just like all the other concepts we've spoken about, in your self-awareness and keep them there. When they show up, you will know them for what they are. You won't fall for them for much longer. You'll see them as excuses that will kill all your plans and keep you from following through.

Get to know your excuses, but don't believe them.

You know the drill. You set your alarm, you make a familiar excuse, and bingo, your plans for the gym are dead. You say, "I am going to put in five job applications," then the excuses come and you play video games instead because you feel you deserve a break since you put in a few yesterday. Excuses are momentum killers, and they are very different from needing to pivot or create a better plan. They get you out of things, they don't move you toward things.

If you took the time to get to know your excuses, I applaud you. All this assessing can feel heavy. I get it. I assess every day, or try to, and my excuses can still win out, but stick with me. Take each of these sections slowly.

You now have a solid list and understanding of the excuses you like to make. It is all awareness; it is all good.

Scarcity

Failure, laziness, and our pet excuses all combine to make life feel scarce. So, what do we end up doing? We hold onto whatever we can. When we are stuck, we can't see new opportunities; we feel scarce and so we invest in whatever we have that makes us feel successful and we don't look back. No one wants to feel bad. So, video games, substances, or an old flame become our focus. We run to these things because life feels scarce, and in scarcity mindset we make really piss-poor choices. Our plans are built on scrambling for some, any type of success, and we can't see opportunity worth a damn.

I have to just simply ask, does your life feel scarce?

Can you follow that string on the ground to the experiences that are making you feel like there are no opportunities? What are they? Take them through the skills you've learned thus far. See those experiences for what they are: scarce.

How?

You know the drill. When I am in full-on coaching mode with someone, I have one goal in mind:

Gather all the insights I can for them, so they see them clearly. Then my goal is to help them stick, to stay in their self-awareness. Stuck there, they become filters, and new information and data will pass through all those insights and then ideas of change are more easily seen.

So, what does scarcity feel like for you? What memories and messages are there? And what does it lead you to do that is unhealthy? Ready for a more abundant view of life?

Breathe. We are still laying the foundation for truly sticky plans.

Anti-Anti

I want to explore with you a trend I am seeing as I converse with those younger than me. It is an interesting conversation that I am hearing more and more. I can sum it up succinctly: the way everything is set up just really sucks.

Normally in these conversations I hear about how awful a nine-to-five job is, or how paying rent is so last-century. I get it. I do. We have a culture, systems, bureaucracy, red tape, school, internships, menial jobs, and also jobs that produce an incredible amount of stress but also, at times, profound meaning.

There is humanitarian work to do, politics to be debated, ideas, tons of ideas. Ideas/messages are at the base of all of this! Remember, we are all just a sum of the ideas/messages we cherish. It is the same for our culture and systems: all ideas, one building off another, some tested, others untested. Democracy was a risk—so many new ideas back then, all untested. Those ideas have morphed and changed. We have what we have now and parts of it, or much of it, might not make sense to you. That is okay.

But I don't want the anti-everything mentality to take you over too much. You have to determine how much of your feeling stuck is based on how you see the systems and structures around you. Even if you completely disagree, one hundred percent, you can find a unique and powerful path forward. It is possible. Structures and cultures change because people change collective ideas.

You change because you take good ideas—better ideas—and you make them your own. But the anti-everything mentality stalls all progress and keeps you in a negative state of mind.

Change what you don't like; don't just complain or give up. Come up with better ideas.

I'm being firm here only because these ideas can really take root. As we assess more and more of these negative aspects of our lives that could get in the way, I hope above all else that they are enlightening. As we get the lay of the land here, the idea is to acknowledge what we are truly dealing with, maybe for the first time. From this knowledge, we will build plans that stick—I'm throwing a ton into your field of self-awareness so you know exactly what and who is in charge of your decision-making.

Don't be a victim, against everything; just find your lane, and it will work out. Plans can still be made even if things don't make total sense to you or appear unfair.

Struggle City, California

As I dive into another story, I want you to understand that, even though this story highlights an extreme, the discussion is really about balance.

How do you find a balance? I wish there was an easy formula here. Trust me, I've tried to create one!

I'm going to bring up lots of things in this story that can throw off your balance.

I can only give you a few questions to ask yourself as you assess those things that can stall us.

Are your plans sticking now? Are you moving forward? Do you feel overly dependent on any of the things we bring up here to bring you balance?

Data. Data that tells us if things are in balance or not. Acknowledge truthfully where you are at.

Now Meet Mike

As the morning set in, I was getting more frantic. I had been searching for the better part of an hour for Mike. All the usual spots around Santa Cruz bore no fruit. I couldn't search all day, but I was really hoping for a miracle. I decided to grab a sandwich at a local deli I knew on a popular shopping street. It was there that I found Mike. High, in and out of consciousness, on a park bench. I shook him awake, and it took him a moment to recognize me. When he did, I saw shame and, for a brief moment, I felt bad for searching for him. I bought him a sandwich, and he could barely talk through his high. He was in a bad spot.

So was I. Remember that my own traumas don't allow me to give up on people easily. I've been called a bulldog in business and coaching. If you become part of my tribe, it is a lifelong commitment whether you signed up for it or not.

Mike and I were both in Struggle City. I was trying to reach him, and hoped he'd hop in the car with me right then and I could take him to a rehab to detox and get back on track. I wasn't getting through at all. As his high released, he became more coherent and lucid. Even then, no dice. He asked me for some money for a hotel for a couple of nights and then waited for my reply.

This isn't a story about drugs.

But you do need to assess your relationship with substances, including technology—anything external to you that you invite into your life. I have been in too many debates with young people who want to pro-and--con to death their use of substances and technology. I don't want that for this discussion.

I just want you to be honest with yourself at this moment. Are substances and technology, including video games, pornography, endless doomscrolling, and fear of missing out online, keeping you from making plans that stick?

Even if your answer is, well, maybe 10 percent of the time, I would probably quadruple that percentage and still feel comfortable about winning a debate with you.

You have to remember and be clear and honest with yourself. You invite these things into your life. They touch on natural predispositions and traumas. They numb us and keep us from living lives that we are fully in charge of. In the end, that is what we need to be successful with our plans: we need to be in charge and in control as much as we possibly can. Of late, my fellow planners, I have lost too many of you to these powerful and addicting externalities. I truly hate my phone's contact list at times. When I scroll to look someone up, I pass by names of people in my tribe who I have lost to substances and complications from technology, like bullying, low self-esteem, and lack of connection. It can feel like a graveyard—each name and their text conversations are a reminder that what we face out there when making our plans stick is no joke, and we should never treat lightly what we decide to invite into our lives.

Please, be aware and be careful with what you invite into your life, especially some of these ideas and concepts we have been assessing.

Back to Mike.

Risk Appetite

As we were sitting in my car in front of a sleazy motel near the Santa Cruz boardwalk, Mike was begging me to pay for a few more nights. I knew he was there to crash with some friends. If I paid for a few more nights, they'd have the funds to go and get a few more highs for everyone. If I gave Mike cash, he'd be bringing the party favors. Damned if I do. The conversation was getting emotional, maybe even a little heated. I couldn't do it, but I kept asking him to stay in the car with me. I told him I would go into the room and grab what little stuff he owned, and we would take the Pacific Coast Highway back to LA. We'd stay in my favorite town, Cambria, and get a good meal. He could shower up while I went through all his stuff and got rid of any paraphernalia and extras. We could work on getting him clean.

I tried to paint a good time. We'd take longer to get to LA. We'd make some stops. I would help him detox. I was throwing out everything, hoping something would stick. You see, this wasn't the first time I'd been in this situation with Mike. Even the conversation felt repetitive.

I finally just had to ask him to take a risk with me, on me, to trust that I knew a little better than him at that moment and could see a little further.

I asked him to take a big leap. I promised him the risk would be worth it.

Are you a risk-taker? Are you willing to take a risk on all this, and on yourself?

I feel, in a way, that I am having the same conversation with you all right now that I did with Mike. Every assessment might feel like a risk. Something risky to possibly give up. Getting all this data can be hard. But will you, can you, take the risk? Will you give these things up for better opportunities? Be honest and assess.

We are also contending with the many labels that get thrown around when someone is struggling or stuck. I don't know your particulars, but I am sure, like all of us, you want something better for yourself. You don't need more labels, and everyone else's fears and anxieties, forced on you. You want a life, a good life, but things are getting in the way. We've gone over some of the major things I have seen getting in our way. There are probably more that are personal to you, but in review, before we start building a foundation for plans that stick, let's list them all out.

If you still feel like there are more things in your way, you now have some helpful tools to assess what is going on with you at a deeper level.

Let's recap some of the things we've assessed:

1. Our memories and their messages
2. Our traumas, big and little
3. How we get our dopamine
4. Our pet cognitive distortions
5. Our failures
6. Our laziness
7. How scarcity affects the way we see life
8. Our view of culture and the structures around us
9. Substances and technology
10. Our appetite for risk

These ten assessment points will give you a better view and lay of the land. They aren't meant to be cute or easy to digest. They are meant to be thought through deeply and not skimmed over. With this knowledge comes power; your ability to keep these ten things in your self-awareness will allow you to more quickly catch who is in the driver's seat, and you get to decide whether you are okay with who that is. I hope it will be you, over time, with deliberate practice.

Mike wasn't ready to let me be in the driver's seat for a bit. He couldn't take that risk. We sat in the car, afternoon rain gathering on the windshield, and we began to say our goodbyes. He hadn't gotten to the point where his current situation felt riskier than starting anew and fresh. His baseline was a quick high and then walking around Struggle City, trying to find the next one. It would take jail and a long road trip with me to finally get him to take a risk on something new, but eventually he got there.

I am hoping you are there now. What is at risk if you aren't?

The ten concepts we've discussed are barriers to success. They put you at risk if not understood and changed. For paths to open and plans to stick, you must be in charge of these aspects of yourself. They are part of all of us.

I am including a formula here on how to take a risk, especially on changing hard things about yourself.

Here is a formula about risk:

Is the risk necessary? (yes or no, meaning does it feel important?) +

evaluate all options (don't be impulsive, actually plan) +

evaluate your capacity (strength/skills, we will get into this next) +

create one small step to take (don't bite off too much) =

chance to evaluate and test (this is how we get data) & finally rinse and repeat, biting off small and steady chunks!

This is how plans stick. This is a life in balance.

Courtesy of the author

Strengths

You have strengths, unique to you, strengths to build from.

I will help you do that in the coming section. I will teach through story and actionable items. It continues to be the best way to go about all this.

Freshman Football

Growing up, I loved sports. I played just about every one of them on organized teams. And I was good at them, athletic and obsessed with going to games and following my favorite players. You wouldn't know that now. I don't think any of my friends would say I was a sports fanatic. I don't get invites to watch a game—not out of exclusion, I just don't think anyone sees me that way. It's too bad, because I still really love sports.

In high school, I decided to try out for freshman football. I made the team. My experience with football before those tryouts was positive, and I felt I was good at it. I played a lot more basketball and baseball. Soccer, oddly, was forbidden. I guess it was seen as a girls' sport when I grew up. I have had my butt kicked too many times playing soccer around the world; I'm truly sad I never picked it up. I digress. Back to football.

Freshman year hadn't started, but football practice and hell week had. The typical high school position-jockeying had begun. Everyone is trying to find their position and then trying to be the best at that position. There was a ton of competition, and I wasn't used to it. Without ego, I never really competed for positions on past teams. I was naturally good at some things, and I usually played a pivotal role on the team. I won basketball championships and other major trophies. Sports always felt like home, and I always found success.

That wasn't so for me in freshman football. I was given positions, but I was always third string, there were always a couple of better players in front me. I wasn't used to that. What I didn't realize was that life was asking me to assess my level of competitiveness and drive to do better. I went to practice and left feeling defeated. Instead of pushing myself, I began to slowly give up and into the feelings of defeat and weakness in my head. Thinking about it now can still be raw for me.

In games, I would get very little field time. No real dopamine hits or sense of accomplishment. I wasn't bonding well with the team, and every day, after lunch and in my last period before practice or a game, my stomach would turn in knots, and I wouldn't want to go to practice or the game. I was totally stuck.

I wish I had had someone pull me aside early on and assess my strengths. I know most of us can feel we have to go at it alone, or we really have no other choice, when we might just not have the support system we need.

What if you could ask a mentor to come alongside you tomorrow? How would you ask them to support you? How could they hold you accountable?

Write down those answers; they will help guide you in future sections.

Eventually, my coach did that with me, but it wasn't before I had hit rock bottom with the team and wanted to quit entirely.

When the coach and I had a chat about what I was feeling and wanting to do (quit before season's end), we honed in on some things I was good at on the field.

He was:

1. Honest with me, like we need to be with ourselves right now. I wasn't the best tailback. I wasn't *the* fastest, but it didn't mean I wasn't a good tailback or that I wasn't fast.

Here is where one of our cognitive distortions can come in strong. I was totally stuck in black-and-white thinking. If I wasn't the best, then I was the worst.

He also:

2. Had me ask some of the teammates I trusted what they saw in me; he wanted me to ask how they thought I could help the team.

So, I did. And I want you to do the same now.

Finding Strengths You Can't See Yourself Yet

- Who can you call? Or text?
- Tell them you are having a hard time seeing your strengths.
- Tell them this is vulnerable and is hard.
- Ask them to send you or talk you through a few strengths they see in you.
- Listen and write them down.
- Set them aside for now.

We just want to get the ball rolling. But please do this, it will give you a boost and help you when we work together in Create.

My teammates helped me see that I was fast, nimble, and at times fearless on the field. We all knew I wasn't going to be first-string running back, but they said I could play special teams like the devil. I soaked in their feedback.

I could play my small role on the field, and I liked it! My coach chimed in and told me he had noticed at kickoff or return I was usually the first to the ball or to the tackle. He wanted that to become my role and for me to own it.

I remember one game where I made a clutch tackle on a kickoff. We were all celebrating, and Coach was asking who made the tackle. The defensive coach named me in front of the team, and the thumbs-up and smile I got from the coach that game made all the horrible anxiety and failure I felt more than worth it. I had worked off my strengths and wasn't stuck in black-and-white, all-or-nothing thinking. Lesson learned.

I decided not to return to football the next year, which at times I have regretted, but we all have those regrets. I learned valuable lessons, though; I learned to build from my strengths, no matter how small or insignificant they may feel or seem to me or the outside world.

I tell this story because it nicely wraps up the dichotomy between failures and strengths.

I had hit a real low in my life at that time. My confidence was tanking, and with all the other typical teenage BS, I was really struggling. A moment really stands out for me. I tell this part of the story just to emphasize just how low it got for me, so that hopefully you can see yourself in the feelings of stuckness I was feeling at the time.

I have to breathe a lot of adult perspective into this part of my story, and I have found solid evidence that shows I am not the same kid who was struggling all those years ago. This part of my failure story brings up a lot of shame for me.

One afternoon, I just couldn't stomach going to practice. So many things weren't going right. I was struggling with my schoolwork, especially math. I wasn't bonding with the team really at all, and still wasn't putting in the effort to improve and cultivate back the spirit of competitiveness and sportsmanship I had prior to joining the football team. I was in my last-period class, and I couldn't go to practice. My parents both worked; I had no ride home. It was either face myself at practice, or walk the super long distance home, alone, taking side streets and ducking behind trees so no one would be privy to my failures. I chose to walk home. It took forever, and I arrived home at the normal time and evaded any questions about practice. Walking upstairs to my room I felt like a failure, and, in all honesty, I was.

That absence from practice sparked the conversation with my coach about quitting altogether. That conversation went so well. I left feeling possible again and ready to build off my strengths.

Are you ready?

What are your strengths? We need your list now.

I need your honesty and I need you to not judge them or limit them. Your friend/ally has got you started already.

Our adult perspective is simple. You have strengths, things unique to you. I know if you look for it you will find evidence to back those strengths up, however small, and no matter how your brain tries to convince you otherwise.

Although I didn't return to football for sophomore year, I found other strengths to build off of. I found other sports and other avenues to compete, maybe not to the same intensity as when I was younger, but those needs found their outlet in volleyball, track, and other hobbies.

I don't care if the only thing you put down was that you are somewhat funny. Let's go with that.

If you think you are funny, that means you have a personality and that you can observe well and see humor in places other people don't. Which means, in a way, you can read people and situations well. It means you can turn a phrase and make it come together in a way that can elicit a positive reaction from people. People like to be around funny people.

Funny people can create something from nothing. Humor can relieve conflicts and disarm people.

I know you see what I am doing. From one strength, I just used my magic to come up with a dozen other strengths. You have strengths, and just like me in those awful moments during freshman year, I couldn't see my strengths worth a damn, until someone pointed them out to me and helped me build off them. I need you to do the same thing now. As you write down your strengths, I need you to see what branches off from them, what do those strengths really mean for you and your life? What does it really say about you if you are a funny person or a super caring person? Your strengths have adjacent strengths, and we need to own those and build on them.

Strength Building Exercise

So, you've called your friend or trusted person and you've listened to my story.

I am assuming you have a starting list of strengths.

Let's say this trusted person said one of your greatest strengths was your kindness. Don't roll your eyes. We can build off that. No matter how small, insignificant, or dumb you feel the strength is, we can build off it.

Do you believe that you are kind?

Acceptance.

What messages and memories come to your mind when you think about you being a kind person? Write them all down. Sit with them, feel them building you up.

Which of your cognitive distortions comes knocking when you start thinking about this strength? What other negative messaging and mindsets show up? List them too. Know your enemies well and keep them close.

Back to kindness.

Where does this kindness come from in you? Why do you feel it is a strength of yours? Journal about this a bit. Explore you and kindness.

What evidence do you have for this strength? This kindness, list it out as well.

What other strengths come from kindness? Is being a good listener one? Is being able to see a need and fill it one? What is adjacent to kindness?

What are the risks to being kind? Acknowledge them, know that risks exist.

Write down three ways you can practice kindness today. Just as an exploration, see that there are avenues to deliberately practice.

What other activities stem from kindness? Hobbies? Volunteering opportunities? Curiosities?

List three careers or jobs that require kindness. Do research if necessary.

Take a moment now, breathe. See, now you have flushed out a strength of yours. You believe you possess it. You understand what comes from it and what can get in the way of you practicing it. You even have some careers or hobbies to explore that will build off your kindness.

Now you need to set one small goal around this strength to develop it further.

Goal: I am going to stop by an assisted living center and see what kind of jobs are available in places like that. *I just want to see what is out there. I think I can see myself at one of those places. It feels aligned well with who I am.*

Great small goal. Just go and see what's there. Get the information and assess from there.

Rinse and repeat. Every time you invest and care for your strengths, your plans stick a little bit better.

Now call that friend, tell them what you learned about you and kindness. And then take some time as you journal to run each one of your strengths through this simple exercise. You will start to see patterns and pathways as you sit with your strengths.

That's a lot of dopamine and a lot of hope.

Courtesy of the Kaiizen Foundation

Confidence

My failures have helped me immensely in my life. Time has taught me that. It is probably pretty hard to see that if you are feeling stuck like I was way back then. Our strengths need to create confidence, just enough to get us started.

Under a mango tree in Zambia, I remember pushing a kid to the limit of his personal strengths so he could find some confidence. It sounds bad, but it wasn't. This kid had an amazingly tough exterior, but no follow-through. All talk, no game. We were talking under the mango tree, as we usually did after a long day's work on our projects. We were talking about his strengths and what to do about them. I was sick of hearing excuses around the things getting in the way of his plans. I immediately had him stand up on a chair and begin screaming aloud his strengths. I wanted them to be real, I wanted him to believe in them, and I wanted him to let everyone around him know what he was capable of. Very Hollywood, I know. It really was. He screamed his strengths, and people started agreeing with him, clapping, and cheering him on. It was a powerful moment. He found confidence in his strengths that day. He was validated, just like I was by my coach and team when I made that clutch play. He sat down, probably believing for the first time that his strengths were real, and then we were able to have an honest conversation about what he should do next.

Your strengths need your confidence, and your confidence will create momentum. Life probably feels slow; you probably don't feel a lot of momentum. That is understandable and it can also be changed.

I have a daily practice I would like to suggest here. It helps keep us focused, and that focus helps us maintain our momentum.

It's analog. Big surprise. You'll need 3x5 cards, and you'll need to set aside some time. Head to a coffee shop or make some tea and get settled at the dining room table.

Meditation Cards

On the front of each 3x5 card you use, I want you to write a category of something important to you, like the priorities you've established or want to establish. It's okay if you establish a few here, right now. You can also be general. It could be a significant other. Or you might just write habits, or another goal you have and want to accomplish.

Some of my cards say:

- My sons
- Surfing
- One of my companies
- Exercise

To name a few. For right now, the backs are blank.

Every morning, I review my meditation cards. I sit with them. I think about whether I am giving them the time and energy they need. I then ask myself, what am I doing this week to invest in this card? Or another way to do it, what can I do this week to move this card forward? I then write ideas I get on the back. After I have reviewed all the cards and put any ideas I've had into my phone as calendar items or onto my to-do list, I put the rubber band around the cards and set them aside until the next morning.

Why does this work so well?

Focusing every morning on what is important to you, feeling those cards, thinking about them, and writing some ideas down is powerful. You feel in charge. Being in charge fills you with confidence.

It also creates easy and inspiring action items, and those create momentum, which creates more confidence and then more momentum. It is a simple process, one I want you to be a part of. It teaches you how to build slowly off your strengths and priorities. I really love it and can't recommend it more highly.

Build confidence. You are worth it.

Forecasting

This is more of a skill, but there is a concept wrapped up in it, like all things.

Forecasting is the ability to take information you have and use it to see the future a bit. It isn't magical; it's a variation of evidence-based thinking. It's taking all that evidence and saying, "What does this say I will do?"

And that's the million-dollar question, especially when getting unstuck and making new plans. We need to base our plans on our strengths and the evidence we have to back them up.

Remember talking about kindness and the different opportunities that can come from kindness? Let's go through another exercise, using kindness as a strength again.

How does having kindness as a strength forecast into plans—maybe a job, or a jump up the career ladder, or even a better relationship?

This exercise requires some thinking. Say we see a job posting that catches our eye. It's a project manager position at a consulting firm. The project deals with the problem of aging nursing homes in the US. You'll be expected to lead a team and gather data on the failures of the current system. You'll do interviews. You'll run numbers. You'll need to present solutions and then move onto the next project.

I don't want you to get lost in the details here so keep up with me.

Here is another way to look at your strengths: they are filters. Things like air and liquids pass through filters. Your strengths become filters you pass information and opportunities through. If the information and opportunities play to your strengths, then you can feel confident they'll have a better chance of passing through all your filters and sticking.

Here we go, briefly:

Kindness would have bearing on many parts of that job posting. The population and industry you are researching needs a kind and thoughtful eye. People who are kind care about the details, care about feelings. So, it already feels like a natural fit. Teamwork can be challenging. Kind people listen, they don't react; they may seem quieter, but that doesn't mean a kind person can't lead. Kindness will no doubt help in your interviews. Kindness will give you perspective as you look for solutions.

We thought a little and used kindness as a filter to see whether this job would play to our strengths. From kindness, we were able to forecast other skills and strengths that kind people possess.

We can use this exercise to forecast whether this job would be a good fit.

I think it does. No job listing will ever be perfect. Same with sorting through college acceptance letters or trying to find a hobby to help us build momentum; it's not one-size-fits-all. Having these filters helps.

You are becoming more familiar with your strengths. Use them as a filter for what comes your way, and you'll make better decisions and plans. I would bet on it.

So, this is how we can forecast whether our plans make sense and will stick. Take an idea, pass it through your strength filters, review the evidence, and see if you feel confident taking the risk to move forward.

Forecasting is an amazing tool. We are just using forecasting to see more clearly and to motivate us, not stall us out. You can use forecasting in relationships, with your goals, with routines you are trying to establish; it will become very helpful as we let this book play out.

Creative Envisioning

I learned this helpful tool from my love of sports as a kid. I remember hearing about some professional basketball team who would spend time envisioning themselves making every free throw or lay-up. They would practice in their mind repeatedly until the action was so familiar in their mind that it just came out naturally in real life.

They called it creative envisioning, and I feel it is an exercise that builds off our strengths and helps us after we have forecast that a certain opportunity looks good for us, that it aligns well.

This is another form of meditation. It requires time and consistency. It requires a quiet, distraction-free place.

How I creatively envision:

Say you've found a hobby like rock-climbing. I am not much of a rock climber, so I won't get all the details right here.

Say you've tried it a few times and feel you are clear on what you need to improve. Maybe that is you learning to place your fingers better on certain grips, ledges, or cracks.

Sit down. Instead of getting anxious about what you don't do well right now, close your eyes and envision yourself on a climb you are somewhat familiar with. Your imagination will fill in the gaps. Imagine yourself doing the ascent. You see yourself making the proper steps to climb up the route. You teach your brain what you'd like your fingers and hands to do in that situation the next time you are in it. And then you keep climbing and keep getting your brain familiar with what you need and want from it when you are climbing.

If you do this consistently, just like my basketball heroes, your brain will see the opportunity to do what you've been practicing in your mind, and it will feel comfortable following through.

This can be used for practicing for an interview, a presentation, or asking someone on a date.

It is changing your brain and training it on how to show up when the opportunity arises.

It is a powerful exercise to build into your daily routines, and it doesn't have to take a long time.

Short-Term Confidence

Have you ever felt a burst of momentum? Like, one day, you just wake up and have the energy to make your bed, run some errands, maybe hit the gym, and do a few other things that make your day feel meaningful and productive?

It probably feels like it was out of nowhere. Totally random and possibly a fluke. What happened?

In my experience, as I have sat and listened to stories of random days filled with fun and productivity, I always ask, what thought did you decide to grab onto that day that was different from all the others racing around in your brain?

Invariably, I hear:

- I was just sick of feeling this way;

- I had an idea about a thing I wanted to do; and

- The day just felt more possible.

Granted, there are chemicals at work in your body, and a good night's sleep helps, too, but I can almost guarantee you had a quick thought, and this time, you chose to believe it, to see things just a little bit differently, and that made all the difference.

To me, that is a burst of short-term confidence that then creates momentum. It is like a gift. It shows us what is possible. We are going to need more of those as we dive into how to create plans that stick, how to follow through better, and ultimately how to show up in this world in the way you want to.

The more you notice these short-term bursts of confidence and momentum, the better you will get at capitalizing on them, building on them, and creating more and more momentum for yourself.

But, as I said, it starts with all those thoughts in your head and which ones you decide to believe. In short, I am trying to talk to you about mindset, which we will dive into more, but mindset starts with which thoughts we decide to latch onto and what kind of world that creates for you.

Want more of them? Check in on your mood. How would you describe your mood now? If there's some negativity in how you are describing your mood, then you aren't creating the right mindset and environment for these short-term bursts of confidence. Checking in often means a better chance at keeping things positive.

Positive mindset = momentum

Opportunity

I can illustrate this better by talking about opportunity.

You may say BS, but there are opportunities all around us. Remember when I tried to inspire all those kids in India? Most didn't have a dollar in their pocket or running water at home. How can I say there is opportunity all around when situations like that exist, and you yourself might feel like you've exhausted all your options?

I love this question. It is raw and real and gets to the heart of this section.

In this section I have tried to have you assess and start to see the reality of your situation—you know, the memories, the messages, the concepts and ideas that take root and paint our worlds. We are truly a sum of these thoughts, messages, and ideas. Josh Brazier is Josh Brazier due in part to my DNA, how my village raised me, but also what I chose to believe and how I've been thinking about my life up to this point.

Just like when we add up all our dopamine, if you take the time to add up all the thoughts that have created your worldview, it will paint a clear picture of why we are who we are. Take a moment to paint that picture for yourself. Think about the prevailing thoughts that you truly believe about yourself. Do you like the person they have created? Do you want to continue to be that person?

We can change—science, neuroplasticity, new habits, different thoughts, and deliberate practice come together to help you get to where you want to go. Even if, right now, you aren't sure where the destination is.

But I need to drive my point home now. If we are stuck, truly stuck, we need to honestly admit to ourselves that we probably haven't been noticing many opportunities around us. We just can't see them. We are blocked from noticing because our frame of mind and mindset is to not see them. We only see where we are stuck, and all the other negative thoughts and emotions that are swirling around in our heads. Those, as we have learned, along with those crazy cognitive distortions our brains love, create filters for what we choose to see and interpret from all the information being thrown at us. I guarantee you have missed some cues or signals. Opportunity has knocked at times, but our filters wouldn't let us hear it. We couldn't see it all for what it was.

Prasanth, the kid who called me out, got what I was trying to say. He wasn't in the best of situations, but he began to see opportunities beyond the more negative filters he had previously seen life through. He saw opportunity in a menial, low-paying job. He took it. He worked hard and it sucked. He told me at times that he wanted to quit. Cleaning up after people at restaurants was messy; he often wanted to walk away from it because it just didn't seem worth it. His brain was screaming for the baseline of being at home and wallowing about his lack of opportunities in life. He wanted to go back to that comfort, but he stuck at it.

One day, he saw someone selling cell phone cases on the street. He saw the guy make a sale or two from the window of his workplace. He thought, I wonder how much he makes on each case. A random thought, a more negative filter, might have turned it into jealousy or something. But no, he stayed curious. He kept the thought positive, and he told me it gave him a little boost at work that day.

He contacted a friend, and they agreed to find out where to buy cases wholesale. His friend wasn't working, so he had some time to investigate. Prasanth gave him some of his hard-won rupees to buy some minutes on his cell phone and maybe a rickshaw ride if needed. He took the risk.

When they figured out the costs of the cases and other items they could sell, they hatched a plan. His friend Raja immediately saw the opportunity, and I was told he quickly got a job instead of wallowing like he had been before. Raja told me that once he saw the opportunity, life just looked different. I loved that. Short-term confidence boost there.

They didn't have the money to just buy a hundred cases and start selling. They both worked and saved for six months to buy their first offering. They were smart. They didn't just fantasize about being rich overnight. They gave it some good thought and made real plans. They researched and anticipated when new phones would be coming out, and they planned around that. They also realized they needed to differentiate themselves from the other vendors and pick good locations to sell from. Lastly, they asked themselves, "Can we get our wholesale guy to get us unique or cool designs that differ from what is out there?" They could, for a little bit more, but they were available! With momentum, confidence, and knowing what they knew about themselves and their situations, coupled with the new, positive filters they'd set up, they began to see opportunity all around.

Remember, it took six months of Prasanth washing dishes and Raja doing street maintenance for them to even get started. Then the day came to order the cases and other items, and they both got cold feet. What else could they do with the money? Dates with girls, a bike, a lot of options came racing through their minds. They resisted—which you will need to do as well. That's your brain again, trying to find something less vulnerable, easier, and less likely to fail.

Today those two have a little shop. I am so proud of them. It took time. Effort. Checking in with themselves and constantly figuring out who or what was in the driver's seat. They had to be vigilant and deliberate, but they are small business owners now. Life is possible.

Our filters will either allow or deny opportunity to be seen. Capital-T truth.

Here is a formula to apply around opportunity:

Know what you're good at/like (play on those strengths!) +

keep it all in your awareness (don't forget, stay present) +

look around (contacts & what others are doing) +

act quick/often on an idea (don't give yourself time to overthink) +

fail fast (don't be afraid to fail either) =

seeing if an opportunity will stick

Prasanth's and Raja's story was meant to inspire and highlight the above formula. Yes, they took risks, yes, they made a good team, and yes, there was a little luck on their sides, but I swear you are no different. Whether it is a business, an educational goal, or just getting into better shape, it will take work, risk, and belief.

Risk big, please.

Lastly, Fantasy

In the coming sections we dive into dreaming big while getting real about your goals. Less stories, more exercises. I don't want you to feel bad for getting amped and dreaming up big stuff. Not at all.

I also can't tell you how often I put the cart before the horse, as they say.

Meaning, I'd get an idea, love it, want to go for it, and instead of working on it, I look up the Ferrari I will buy when I am successful, or the sailboat I'll travel the world in. I end this section with fantasy thinking because I know just how distracting and harmful it is. I have had to make extreme efforts to curb this tendency in myself and just get to work.

The story of Prasanth and Raja had some subtle points I'd like to elaborate on for a few here.

It is so easy to see an opportunity, love it, and be curious about it, and then start thinking, *we are going to be the world's next billionaire, Oscar or Grammy winner, or tech CEO.* You can (and I want that for you!) but getting lost in fantasy thinking skips a whole lot of steps and then creates huge expectations that will ultimately crush the opportunity. I have learned this the hard way, but it wasn't always the case for me.

Wealth in my family came and went. We had years of incredible abundance and times when we were all pitching in to cover family expenses. It was volatile and, at times, very scary.

It took some time to really understand the messages those memories created in me and the resulting filters that painted how I saw life. It all created some heavy, heavy mindsets.

The lean times created a strong work ethic. At times, honestly, there was no other choice. When I graduated high school, my parents had just started a new business; there were no extra funds. I worked all summer and saved enough to be able to move out of state with friends. I wanted so badly the college experience. My dad drove us in our car to my new apartment that I put down the deposit on, that I helped furnish. He bought me my first load of groceries, and then life was totally on me. My other friends from back home did have it easier. Some had everything paid for; they had their car and college tuition covered. I could have been feeling a range of emotions toward them, but I kept them at bay. I was going to take a semester to save up for school and then start in January. I worked three jobs, often on the same day. I would work at a call center really early, which taught me a lot about working a job you liked. I'd take the bus home, eat lunch, then walk over to the car wash for the afternoon shift. I would then eat a dinner of ramen and toast and head to an office building to work as a janitor. I was able to move up at the car wash and quit the call center (never quit until you have a better opportunity, please; it helps with momentum). I saved and saved. I was still social, had fun, but I went to bed exhausted at night. I paid my rent, I covered my bills, and I felt really good.

In the end, though, I didn't save enough to attend college the next semester. While I was home over Thanksgiving break, a friend's dad offered me an opportunity after hearing about all the work I had put in. It would be manual labor, more hard work, but I had built up the muscle of work ethic and it was starting to pay off.

It did feel like I had failed, but I stayed positive, which let me continue to see new opportunities. I had momentum.

Weren't we talking about fantasy thinking?

Here we go. I worked that manual labor job doing demolition on pools. Up every morning at five a.m., at the yard picking up my truck and crew, and off to the job site for a long day of jackhammers, wheelbarrows, and dirt. I worked hard. Every day. It felt so good (we will get into this together too). I worked that job for a year, often proving to myself and to my boss that he could rely on me to get the job done and that I could rely on myself to want to do hard work.

Then another opportunity came my way.

There was this amazing man who took me under his wing. It was the same story. He saw how hard I worked, and he was helping me formulate my goals and plans. He was funny, compassionate, but tough. He was successful, and I have always found that with success comes an ability to be blunt with people sometimes. Sometimes he would tell me something and he would laugh, but I wanted to cry. Not really, but you get the point.

He offered me a job. It paid extremely well. It was different work than doing demo on pools in the hot Los Angeles sun. I wanted to impress him, so I continued to work hard, really hard.

Then I slipped. The big paychecks made me comfortable, made me overly confident. I just started to notice I would make excuses for myself more. If the work got hard, I didn't find solutions, I started to find excuses. Looking back, I can simply say I got comfortable, and now let's get into that.

An Important Bridge to Cross: the Discipline of Discomfort

There are never any truly easy fixes.

You will be uncomfortable. Any time we try and shift mindsets, reach for new goals, or let go of the messages that don't serve us, we will experience lots of discomfort. It is a vulnerable discomfort; it can feel quite lonely.

This book could be providing you with a certain type of discomfort. I haven't suggested easy, quick fixes thus far; I, in a way, am theorizing that true change can't be had quickly. You can make progress quickly, no doubt, but the mindset changes I'm asking of you require work, sacrifice, and time.

Life, as many have shouted from many a rooftop, is all about compromises and tradeoffs. One thing must give for another to get. This idea naturally brings us to the idea of fairness.

Fairness—let's be honest with ourselves—is nothing more than a replacement word for being comfortable. Recent arguments around fairness have become heated and distracted. I am not talking about equity or equality here; I am simply exposing a trap we all face when it comes to change. The trap that everything needs to be fair for us to get started on ourselves, or to take advantage of an opportunity. We know life is not fair. I doubt it ever will be for any of us. We have worked hard as a society to make things more equitable, but I don't want to plant false hope. Waiting for all things to be even to get started is just us not wanting to be uncomfortable.

In our earlier discussion on baseline, we exposed the idea that our brain wants to be in a comfortable spot and will fight against any idea to the contrary. We just don't want to be uncomfortable in any way, and we deeply personalize things when we are. It becomes an offense, not an opportunity, and we all suffer because of this mindset.

Discomfort = growth. We know this. Discomfort is a signal. You are hungry, you eat. You don't like where life is going, you start to change course. Uncomfortable and uneasy feelings can be your friends. They don't have to be ignored and build until they boil over. You can befriend discomfort if you choose. It can become quite the symbiotic relationship, working off each other for each other's greater good. It's true, no BS.

I could write for days on the many culprits of our need to be comfortable, to never suffer an inconvenience, or really to ever suffer at all. I will try to illustrate a couple of moments where discomfort turned into learning and learning produced growth.

I was at this silent retreat many years ago in the hills of Santa Cruz, California. The settings were ideal, the outdoor showers were out of this world, and the food was so nourishing and comforting. There were a lot of us there; I had even brought some friends. At the beginning of the retreat, as we learned about the place, what we'd be doing, and what the real rules were, I kept thinking to myself, there are so many lovely people here I want to get to know, I don't want to stay silent. But silent we had to be. We were allowed to speak when answering questions, but other than that, silence. Some participants would give an answer and all I wanted to do was ask them more questions about themselves and their lives. I even found myself dropping little morsels about me in my answers so I could signal to people that when all this was done, I was open to getting to know them.

Being silent became more uncomfortable as the days passed. I started seeing all these parts of me that were becoming very, very uncomfortable. I wasn't being validated. I wasn't being social. I had to be with my thoughts, and the person I was getting to know wasn't a very comfortable person to be with.

I imagine it is the same for you.

Change—feeling forced by life, parents, society, whoever, to change—is very uncomfortable. But there is a discipline to the discomfort. Honestly, it may be one of the most important decisions you make before you embark on the journey we are going to go on together in the next few sections of this book.

Can you tolerate this type of discomfort? The type that keeps you in tune with your current moods and mindsets? Can you keep at things even when progress feels slow? Can you not expect a quick fix?

We've all been doing a disservice to ourselves with this relentless need to be comfortable. Just think about our lives right now. We hardly have to lift a finger, and most of our suffering comes from things we want, mainly because most of our needs are met by technology, society, and others. Own this, don't fight it. We all have situations and things in our lives that I know we'd trade away in a heartbeat. I am not negating those things. I am asking you to ultimately assess your relationship with being comfortable and therefore avoidant toward change and all the fears of the unknown and discomfort that come with change.

As I sat in silence that long weekend, as I hiked in silence, I had a realization. I had no validating outlet for my emotions. With my emotions and feelings locked inside, I became very uncomfortable, uneasy, and untethered. In a weirdly profound way, I came to realize my emotions and the feelings they created in me, once not allowed to be expressed so openly, screamed to be let out, to be in charge. It was scary and enlightening because I came to see how powerful they were, yet how completely full of shit they were. They were so all over the place, so random, so triggered by unusual and petty things, it almost became comical watching them whizz and fly by.

Like when they ran out of the tahini sauce for my salad or when I realized the hummus was not homemade at the retreat. It was WWIII in my mind. We'd have chores to do during the day, and at times I felt above those tasks; didn't they know who I was? What I've done with my life? Thoughts that created these strong emotions, and those emotions would create feelings of having to do something about what I was thinking. Which over time created mindsets, outlooks, and patterns of behavior. Being silent at that retreat allowed me to see my mindsets play out inside me. The evidence was clear. I did not want them in my life. Change was going to be uncomfortable. I had to embrace the discipline of discomfort if I wanted to stand a chance.

I Slipped

Stick with me here. Remember that awesome opportunity I got with that mentor who took me under his wing and gave me a job? It paid so well at that time in my life. I told you I slipped, and it became one of the biggest lessons in my life on how certain thoughts can create emotions that make you act and feel differently.

I really had slipped, and I lost my strong work ethic for a while. I started thinking grander thoughts. A few more bucks in your packet can do that to you. It wasn't about the money—money does change us, but I think it amplifies who we already are. Sorry, let's get back on track here.

I slipped because I accepted that life should be about me being more comfortable and that it should somehow be my mind's goal never to have to dig a ditch or work in the hot sun again. I grabbed hold of a few thoughts my mind cooked up, like, *wouldn't this be nice*, or *I deserve this*, or *this is beneath me* (fantasy thinking). My success in life seemed to water the beliefs these thoughts had created in me so long ago.

I started fantasizing about the fruits of my labor instead of loving and focusing on the work.

That idea is not mine. It is an immortal philosophy expressed in the *Bhagavad-Gita*: *to the work alone thou hast a right, not to the fruits.*

So, to tie this all up, fantasy thinking ultimately stems from our need for comfort or our desire not to be uncomfortable. It is the ultimate momentum killer because it is all in our heads, and we can make ourselves comfortable up there.

I need to tie all this together because I have many ideas and stories that I want to use to help you make the most important of decisions.

I want the changes you want for yourself, but let's not deny that those changes will take real work, and real work is often hard, brow-beating, and uncomfortable. True change can't be phoned in or done through an app, although they can help.

Because I slipped all those years ago, I have had to battle with my relationship with being uncomfortable, and I have had to deliberately embrace the discipline of discomfort. I work at it every day.

I know you can see this in your life. Fantasy about being comfortable produces cheap and false dopamine hits, and we ultimately suffer from the fantasy of it all. We want to be rich, famous, successful, whatever. We dream and we fantasize; our brains love it and begin to crave it. Why work for anything when we can just think, emote, and feel our way to a nice-sized dopamine hit?

I want your plans to stick. Soon, we will begin to visualize and make those plans, but let's commit right now that we know this will be hard work. You will want to give up. You will want to be comfortable. You will want to make excuses for yourself. You will fantasize, think that other people's lives and plans are better and that your life sucks. Your brain will begin a game of tug-of-war between you and your level of comfort.

That's just the way it will be.

Acceptance.

Courtesy of the Kaiizen Foundation

A Story to Bring It All Home

I was in Mexico, driving a fifteen-passenger van filled with a bunch of rowdy and entitled treatment boys. We were doing work at an orphanage and taking a drive to burn a little time and see the beautiful countryside. It had just rained, and everything was green to the max and beautiful. The dirt was dry in the middle of the road and I had to avoid the sides, or we'd get stuck.

As we drove along, all I heard was BS. All the boys were being idiots. They'd be bragging about this, complaining about that, and being super entitled. I'm a super patient person. I wasn't mad. I was just bummed the lessons weren't sinking in. No one seemed to want to work on the construction project we had set up for the day. So, I had an idea. I started drifting slowly, more and more, toward the edges of the dirt road. We started slipping a bit, and some of the boys noticed and whined about what they would do if we got stuck. My door opened. I edged closer and closer, and like clockwork, we slid and got stuck.

The boys started hurling all sorts of complaints and expletives at
me. I smiled. One kid realized I'd done it on purpose.

I said, "Well, it is time to get to work." I stood to the side. I just
expected the boys to get us out of the mess. Some boys threw out ideas,
and a battle ensued for the plan to get us out. They chose one and got
to work. It was dirty, muddy work. The mud was more like clay. It
was slippery, and more than one boy ended up on his back trying
to get leverage with the sticks, rocks, and things they found around
them to help them dig us out and get us some traction. The hard work
was beginning.

More than once, a truck passed by, and they'd have rope and the
ability to get us out in no time. I declined politely and told them the
gringos needed to learn some hard work. They looked at me wryly and
wished us luck. Some stayed to watch. It was an incredible scene.

The group hadn't really bonded yet, but they were starting to. They
were getting dirty and doing a lot of trial and error. I would hop in the
van and try to get us out once they felt they'd solved the problem. Most
of the time, we just got more stuck.

You will feel this way. You will. The boys were getting frustrated,
dirty, and mad.

I was still standing on the side. Here and there, I would poke fun at
one of their ideas. A few times, they hurled mud at me. Luckily, I've got
good reflexes.

Some started blaming me and complaining that we would never get
out. It is easy to blame others when things get hard, I get it.

You'll feel that way, too.

It was starting to get hot, but progress was being made. The van
wasn't out yet; it had been close to an hour. No quick progress here.

I just told them I knew they could do it.

I am saying the same to you. Give yourself time.

Finally, a decent plan was hatched. They synthesized the data. They
took stock of what was not working. They had finally realized that the
van's power was sent to the rear wheels. But going forward meant that

the wheels had to get enough traction to push the whole van out. If they created a plan for the van to go in reverse and pushed from the front and told me how to move the steering wheel, they were sure they'd get out. A stickier plan indeed.

I told the little crowd that had gathered their new plan, and one of the men said, "Finally!" I chuckled. They got it. We were all sure their plan would stick.

They went to work, created a path for wheels with good traction, and asked me to hop in the van. I was hesitant. I didn't want the experience to end. They were doing so well after a long, uncomfortable ordeal. I wanted to stay in that moment of hard work. But they wanted to see if their plan would work, and I wouldn't let them drive the van. Everything I was seeing and hearing was music to my ears.

You, like them, by figuring out and assessing what is getting in the way of your plans, should be just as excited as they were to see their plans in action. Why? They were authentic and hard-won.

I fired Big Blue up and put her in reverse. I asked them to guide me, to tell me about how much gas to give. A group of boys gathered at the front of the van to push. I slowly stepped on the gas, and the van started to find some grip. The boys pushed with all their might; they yelled at me to steer (I knew), and in less than a minute, we were free from the sticky clay mud of that Mexican dirt road.

The boys were ecstatic. High fives everywhere. Cool boys hugged the nerdier ones. The group had bonded. On the drive to the orphanage, I didn't hear any stories about insane shoe collections at home or anything like that; I listened to the details of the battle they had just won. I just drove and smiled. The rest of the trip was incredible. They worked hard and played hard with the kids.

We are all stuck in some way. Hard work, our decision to embrace that and its inevitable discomfort, and a bunch of trial and error will get us unstuck. It will take some teamwork. We will fail and maybe fall face first in the mud, but embrace that.

That is the discipline of discomfort at work. It will serve you well.

Whether it was me becoming so uncomfortable with my thoughts and emotions at that retreat, me realizing just how comfortable I had become and just how much my work ethic had slid, or me getting that van stuck in the mud, I value hard work and you must as well. It is our only way out. Time to get uncomfortable, but don't worry. There are some solid and time-tested ways to create new plans that not only stick, but are authentic to you and what you want for your life.

That is where I started after I realized how much I had slid.

I had to stop fantasizing and start visualizing what my hard work could create for my life. It was a profound moment because fantasy and visualization are so similar. They both produce dopamine, but only one creates real effort. So, as we begin to create, I want to give you permission to convert your fantasies into creative visualizations, and from those visualizations, we will find plans that stick.

But at the end of this section, I will leave you with questions to ponder.

Are you willing to leave your fantasies, your pride, and your feelings of fairness, possible victimhood, and comfort behind to open a new chapter in your life? If something I have brought up or said has stuck with you, dig around. What's so uncomfortable there?

A Formal Bridge to Cross: Executive Functioning Skills

I don't have many letters behind my name or a fancy degree. I don't have a research lab or grant money funding me to prove to you that this process I am sending you through is exact science.

I do have some data, though.

1. 28 percent of students drop out before they even become sophomores.

2. In a recent survey of 17,000 high school students across the US, 42 percent reported clinical symptoms of depression.

3. Around 53 percent of recent college graduates are unemployed or underemployed.

4. Since 2000, the percentage of teens working summer jobs has fallen from 51.7 to 36.6 percent.

5. About 7,200 high school students drop out daily. That means schools are losing three hundred students every hour or five students every minute.

6. General video gaming use among the US population increased significantly during the Covid-19 pandemic. Between May and December 2020, US teens aged fifteen to nineteen years spent an average 112.8 daily minutes on playing games and using computers for leisure, up from 73.8 minutes per day in the corresponding period of 2019. In 2022, the daily time spent on such activities among this age group decreased to 98.4 minutes per day.

7. Total federal student loan debt has roughly tripled since 2007.

8. The average credit card debt in America is $7,951.

9. Over the course of a person's lifetime, they will work on average 90,000 hours.

10. It is estimated that most people will have twelve jobs during their lifetime.

When stats like this exist, I can intuit that things aren't going well for a lot of us. It seems there are more things getting in the way than there are opportunities available. Life is not easy out there.

I meet with people daily. Hours of my day are spent in problem-solving mode, helping people eliminate their roadblocks and find traction through simple skills and concepts.

If you took the time to assess and journal about how each concept shows up in your life, I applaud you, because they aren't easy things to look at. Our brains will create powerful excuses for our current reality and the baseline it is used to and wants to maintain. It is a battle, and it is work, but having those concepts in your self-awareness is key. I promise you will notice more quickly when these concepts and more negative mindsets act upon your life, and you will then be brought to a choice point. Stay the same, or make a different, healthier choice that keeps you on the path to fulfill your goals.

I need to plant ten more formal seeds into your self-awareness. Please stick with this. These are clinical but essential development containers I need you to think about and assess before we start creating. I will put my spin on these containers and give you real-life examples you can relate to. Your plans, as we progress, need to build these skills. Without them, plans fall apart, almost guaranteed. The skills and tools taught later are contained in these concepts. My hope is that, as you move along, you'll be able to label when you are doing an activity that either needs to be done or helps you build these aspects of yourself. Every time I do laundry or clean out the garage, I laugh as I list off all the executive functioning skills I employ. That laugh is more of an acknowledgment. I am progressing, sticking with things because these skills are very real and very necessary to make our plans stick. And don't worry—later in the book, I will teach you direct ways you can implement these skills.

So, this will be your last bridge from Assess to Create, but take great care with these containers. If you really need to improve in one of the areas, then you know very clearly where you need to get to work. Remember, all is well; there is another side of the coin. Let's dive into these essential executive functioning containers.

Ten Essential Executive Functioning Skills

Attention

The ability to focus on a task, person, conversation, or chapter in a book.

How is your current attention span? Would you say your focus is good, or not so good?

My ADHD is a beast to control. I can be talking to someone, have a different thought enter my mind, stop what I am saying, and focus entirely on that thought, leaving the conversation on a cliff. Our ability to focus is key when keeping the concepts and assessments we just went through. We will go through some attention-building activities in Part III.

Planning

Do you have the ability to strategize, forecast, and understand resistance points before you plan?

Do you wake up with a plan, or do you chase the day? Would you say you are proactive with your time, or completely reactive?

I also equate planning to how exhausting the items on my to-do list feel, or how I feel at the end of my day. Usually, when I have been proactive, I feel energized and complete, not exhausted and run into the ground. That is a result of chasing my reactivity to life and its events.

Time Management

It's understanding how much time it takes to do most things, while also allocating your time well.

It is curious, and we will get into this more, but most of us give no mind to how much time things really take, which inhibits our ability to manage our schedules. Time management is knowing that you have a dentist appointment, what time it is, where it is, and how much time it will take to get there, to be in the appointment, then drive or get to the next thing on your calendar. That whole process followed one acknowledgment and decision after another.

How do you do with time management?

Self-Control

As we have previously discussed, it's the ability to control our thoughts, emotions, and feelings.

When we lack self-control, we are reactive and personalize everything. We yell at our alarm clock, get annoyed by traffic, and take someone's rescheduling personally. When in control, we can take in the data and proactively choose how we will react. That is our sweet spot, the ability to stay in control and not complicate things for ourselves.

How in control are you?

Meta-Cognition

This big word essentially means self-awareness—your ability to be aware of your thinking.

When we're aware of our thoughts and surroundings, we make decisions based on that data. When our awareness is low, we react; our feelings, thoughts, and emotions come on quickly, and we go with them instead of processing and proactively deciding what is true and how we want to proceed.

Are you familiar with that part of yourself that holds awareness and goals and keeps them top of mind?

Working Memory

It is being able to recall information while working, talking, etc.

Remembering the gate code or someone's name, where you put your keys or backpack, is not a skill to be taken for granted. It is a muscle we build and maintain. Creating systems for where you put information, your things, helps in this process. This skill is buddy-buddy with our organizational skills. How to tie your shoes and how you fold your towels builds your working memory because they create reliable systems for you to rely on.

How strong is your working memory?

Flexibility

How well do you adapt, pivot, and act when change is needed?

Honestly, this is a key skill to build. As much as we'd like to predict the future, we cannot. We want our plans to stick, but we don't know what will be thrown our way on any given day. This relates as well to how much we personalize change. Do we take an unexpected pivot personally? Do we let it ruin our momentum and turn us into the victim of an unforeseen hiccup? Do we go around complaining about how this one thing just made it impossible for us to see our plans through? If so, this is a great skill to work on.

Perseverance

This is your ability to finish something you have started, even when resistance is high.

We could relate this skill to our previous discussion of hyper-novelty. Our brains want fun, and fun = dopamine. Not everything is fun. Most of life is tedious, and that isn't something you should take personally. Perseverance builds your ability to deal with discomfort consistently. This is you finishing that long chapter in biology, that last mile, or just not snoozing your alarm.

When was the last time you felt you persevered through something?

Organization

This refers to the systems, places, and thought put into the stuff, things, and materials around on a daily basis.

Are you an organized person? Look around your space right now. What grade would you give yourself?

Organization is another word for systems. If you can make your favorite coffee, you can organize your clothes, you can plan a day. Each is just a more complicated system. We start small in Part III, and we build your ability to organize and to stick with it. If we are disorganized, we simply need better systems and to bite off smaller chunks.

Task Initiation

It's your ability to start, mainly your ability to start something independently.

This skill is the domino that makes all the others fall. Can you take an idea in your head and go with it? Can you begin a task? Can you see an assignment on your syllabus and create a plan to start and finish it? If this feels weak, our work later with starts and finishes will be very important for you.

Adulting

Even writing these out made me chuckle a bit. These are ten containers that prove to those around us that we can adult well. What do I mean?

Each one of these ten skills has been drilled into you since kindergarten. Your parents, teachers, bosses, and friends have been hopefully trying to build these skills in you. It is okay if some of them feel weaker than others. Remember, it is just work to be done, and for some of us, like me, with my attention and self-control, these will be lifelong struggles.

Let me be clear. Honestly, these are no laughing matter. If one is off, it can throw off our plans. Remember, none of this is to make us feel bad about ourselves. It is information, and it can empower us to work on and change where we may feel weak. I am confident your plans will stick better the more familiar you are with these skills and the more you embrace where you need to improve. You may feel lazy now. Or you may be addicted to fantasy thinking. Or one of your cognitive distortions may be out of control. If you are aware of it, it means it doesn't have the same grip on you it did before. That should give you a whole lot of hope.

Now we get to have some fun.

To recap:

- Please take each one of the concepts we discussed and mull them over. Take time to assess what you feel about them, how they show up in your life, and if you need to improve, eliminate, or strengthen them.

- Good plans that stick build on your strengths and the momentum they create. Play to your strengths until your confidence catches up.

- Get used to discomfort; see it as a positive step toward growth, not something to personalize and run from.

- Keep what resonates most with you in your self-awareness. See it in your day-to-day plans and interactions with life. Notice things more. The hope is that it will lead you to make better decisions, which equal stickier plans.

- Make it a goal to develop the executive functioning skills we discussed. You can improve! I work at them every day.

What is to come now is a chance to brainstorm alongside me, and remember, there are no bad ideas in brainstorming. Brainstorming is a place to explore without judgment. Nothing is permanent in brainstorming. We will have fun seeing what is inside of you that would like to be expressed and experienced.

Skills to bring to the brainstorming session:

- An open, positive mind.
- Knowledge of the messages/mindsets that are uniquely yours and influence you, your confidence, and your ability to make plans.
- Knowing what gets in your way, and all those concepts we reviewed—know your favorites.
- Your list of strengths.

See you in the next part.

Part II

CREATE

Life in the Margins

We are back in Hawaii now. I was staring at the long piece of toilet paper on which I had written a bunch of ideas, goals, and things I felt I needed to make right. I'm not going to lie: after I wrote it all down, I was on cloud nine and felt I could do anything. After I saw the sunset and came back home, the tide started to shift. I looked it over and concluded I must be out of my mind. I left you all on a cliffhanger a while back. Let me get you off of it now. But before I do, let's be a little ambitious: write in the margins of this book some lofty goals—ones you need to reach for. Let them out without fear or judgment. You have these in you; they are as diverse and lovely as each of us on this planet. Earmark this page.

Like in all our lives, a lot was going on in mine at the time. I was thirty-four and hoping for more. I was thirty-four and feeling pretty disconnected from myself and those around me. Thirty-four and alone again. On that long piece of toilet paper, I set out some goals to help me feel more connected and engaged in life. One of those goals was to become a dad. It was a crazy idea. I was single, thirty-four, coming off my sabbatical, not earning much, and with no stable place to live. I was being my nomad self, and I still enjoyed it. I also still really sucked at relationships.

It is interesting that when you start to imagine things differently (like writing some lofty, stretch goals in the margins), a lot wakes up inside you and around you. I have seen it happen too many times to consider it a coincidence. That is why we have been assessing and clearing the way for opportunity to knock. We've been seeking understanding and clearing the clutter to see things anew.

I acknowledge that everything we are doing together will apply to your unique and diverse situation. I wouldn't write any of this if I didn't feel the principles were universal—not one-size-fits-all, but principles you can ponder and apply to your situation.

At that time, an orphanage my organization had been supporting for many years was closing, which meant all the kids would be relocated. It was going to be a big loss. Thousands of volunteers and I had created incredible memories there. It was impossible to even think about that chapter closing in my life. I had seen most of those kids grow up during the decade we had worked there. It wasn't a sure thing, but like I said, it was one of those issues swirling around in my life at the time. When I got back from Hawaii, I immediately went to my little beach shack in Baja and spent some time at the orphanage. I wanted to get the lay of the land and see what was what. I wanted to make the goals I set in Hawaii more real. I wanted to get started. I didn't want it to be just more fantasy thinking. I felt I gained a lot of self-awareness while in Hawaii, and it was up to me to start some task initiation, some planning, etc.

On a side note, and an important one, when we have inspirational experiences or insightful moments, there really is a small window of time before it all wears off and we are back to our old selves. That is why I have been begging you to do the writing, the brainstorming, and the other activities in this book. I'm creating short bursts of confidence for you, which gets the ball rolling, which we have to take responsibility for and turn into actionable plans. Just acknowledge the very real fact that our window is small after those short bursts of confidence to initiate a task or two. Back to my story.

While at the orphanage, one of my dear friends and employees let me know that an alumnus from the orphanage had just been diagnosed with stomach cancer. He had recently had a kid and was in bad shape.

We went to see him, and the prognosis was not good. We brainstormed what could be done, and it seemed all we could do was make his life more comfortable and try to get him the best care possible. We searched stores for walkers and a more comfortable bed for him. We purchased supplies and tried to support his new wife and son as much as we could. I went down as often as I could.

It was all very heavy. Try as we might, we could never get him access to the medical support he needed. The disease was progressing rapidly. On one trip, we got permission to take his little brother, who was still at the orphanage, to go and visit him. It was probably going to be the last time. It was a sad reunion. As we left, I said goodbye to this amazing kid I'd watched grow up and whose days were numbered. I saw him say goodbye to his brother. I saw them embrace. I went to say my goodbyes, and this new father and husband made me make him a promise. He asked me if I would always take care of his little brother. Maui and my goals flashed into my mind, along with that long piece of toilet paper I'd written on. It read: *I don't need to wait to be a dad anymore.* In making that promise, I didn't realize I had just become one.

I was taught an incredibly important lesson that day: it is not a bad thing to dream big; it is not selfish to want things for yourself. I also learned that sometimes you pick up where another's story ends. I had you write a lofty goal or two in the margins. Refer back to them. Do you really want them? In Maui, setting that goal of being a dad was a lofty goal for me. I still struggle with relationships, even as I write this, but it is a goal of mine to get better, and ten years later, it is burned into my brain. I constantly see opportunities to improve my relationships and take life up on those opportunities. Memorize those lofty goals as we go into our big brainstorm. They will keep your mind open and hungry for something new. These lofty goals bring us a lot of hope.

I don't know what should be on your long piece of toilet paper. I want you to have the courage to jot some things down now if you didn't earlier. Big things, small things. No matter how stuck you feel, I promise you can always create, even if it is from rock bottom. I didn't know how any of those things I wrote down would come true. I think I just believed in my ability to create and work hard. That's all. I didn't have endless funds in the bank. I didn't even know where to start, but I had to trust what I initially felt in those vulnerable moments were the authentic needs and desires I had for my life. I did, and as a result, opportunities started showing up.

Use the margins; there's life in the margins.

That day I made that promise, my perspective changed completely. It was what screenwriters call an inciting incident. It threw me into a new story, and acting was now up to me. Yes, I could run away like I always did, or I could have easily forgotten my promise. That promise had struck a real nerve in me. I wanted something more for my life, and to regain my work ethic and not fear so much. So, I took the promise seriously. I need you to do the same.

Make a promise as well to see your lofty goals through.

It has been amazing to see what has played out since I wrote mine down.

With all this in mind, let's dive into some solid advice now. You are a creative person, a creator. We all are. I can't draw or paint worth a damn, but I have other outlets for my creativity. You do, too, and we are going to start big with your life and its direction because, honestly, it is the best place to start.

You deserve this. It is fun. These plans we are going to start making are going to change. You will have to reassess, pivot, or drop some of them, but the difference is clear. You are more in charge now. Not your emotions. Not the messages from your memories. Not our crazy brains. A more focused and determined you is present now because you know yourself so much better and what you want for yourself, even if all you know are the crazy, lofty goals you wrote in the margins of this book.

Here, now, I will try to give you some unique and just as applicable advice. We are going to start with my favorite exercise.

Key Formula

In the coming sections, I will use words like priorities, bridges, goals, habits, and routines liberally.

Please memorize this formula:

1.   Your priorities (values) are most important here; we build from them.

2.   Clear priorities will build bridges.

3.   Bridges are goals that get you to your bigger goals.

4.   Goals are feedback, ways to assess progress.

5.   As you live your priorities, you create routines.

6.   Those routines become habits.

7.   You become your habits, which hopefully reflect your priorities.

8.   The process is evergreen, meaning it is how you build a life and new mindsets.

Hopefully, you will fall in love with assessing and pivoting, because that is basically life.

Now, with that in mind, we get to have more analog fun.

Poster Board

If you can, put this book down, go to the store, and grab some poster board or a bunch of paper. I want you to write your name in the middle of it and draw a box around it. Get creative now. I am going to give you a bunch of words to scatter across that poster board, and I want you to draw a box around each of those as well. Below are the words, in no particular order. I don't want to invite your mind to become too rigid, I need it open, and you need to keep any thoughts like "This is lame!" out of your mind.

Step 1: Write these in different places on the poster board. I will define them here for you. We will use these terms throughout the book.

- Mindsets: patterns of thought made solid by routine and action, how we then view the world

- Bridges: temporary actions, goals, or considerations constructed to help you achieve larger goals

- Hobbies: ways to practice, find what we love, gain confidence, and build community

- Service: a time out from our own lives while gaining new perspectives and insight serving others

- Third Spaces: places outside of your home where you can create, learn, and build community

- Priorities: your values, your focus, what matters to you

- Routines: activities and tasks we practice to build muscles of consistency and follow-through

- Become: who do you want to become? Not like "a millionaire," but what characteristics do you want to be known for?

- Goals: an action that can be measured clearly to bring you feedback on progress

- Habits: these are formed through deliberate practice and make up who you are

- Mentors: any person, book, or inspirational figure who helps guide and molds your character and plans

Give them space to breathe.

This exercise takes some time. Accept that. The categories I put down in Maui were different but, in a way, the same. I took my friend in Mexico through this exact exercise, so I will lead you through it and use him as an example. These categories are tailored to where you may be and inspired by my decades of coaching. I want to elaborate on each of those ten categories, and then we will dive into the exercise. Stay with me. I promise it will be worth it.

My friend and I made some eggs and chorizo, heated up some tortillas, and squeezed some oranges. I went to the car and gave him a Sharpie and a poster board. He was like, "Oh, you're serious." I told him I was and to write these categories down and give them space to breathe. He did, and as we ate, I explained them to him.

In the beginning, this really is a mindfulness practice. Take a few breaths. Center yourself. Eliminate distractions. Check in on your mood. Are you ready? Grounded? Good. Get into the details on your poster board. Get specific. Don't be shy or lazy.

- Think about your **Mindsets**; write the ones that seem to be in charge.

- What are your current **Hobbies?** Do you have any hobbies you want to pick up again or maybe try?

- Have you done **Service** work in the past? What did you do? How did it push you? Where would you serve now?

- Do you have **Third Spaces** already? Can you think of any in your area? Do your friends or family go to any already?

- What are your current **Priorities**? Can you name them? As you look ahead, big sky/big picture, what are becoming clear and desired priorities for your life?

- What **Routines** do you have in your life now? Do you think they build you up? What are some routines of people around you that you admire? Can you jot down some you'd like to establish alongside your new priorities?

- Who do you ultimately want to **Become**? Do you feel you are on your way? Are there characteristics you'd like to build? Flaws you'd like to do away with?

- As you look over your priorities and values and who you want to become, what **Goals** are becoming more apparent for your life? What would you start focusing on to help you get where you want to go?

- Think about **Bridges** you have used in the past to get you bigger and better things. Write them down. What bridges would you create to get you closer to your bigger goals?

- What do your **Habits** look like now? List them. Do you like the person they create? What would you change? What habits would you like to establish? Have fun, think big here!

- Do you consider anyone a **Mentor**? Make a list. Also make a list of potential mentors. Also write down impactful books, podcasts, and other sources of information and guidance that serve as mentors to you.

Have fun spreading these all over the poster board or on different pieces of paper. Let the definitions sink in. I tried to make them clear. I don't want to overcomplicate the process.

I want you to take some time with these words.

I'll walk you through one here.

Let's say we focus on third spaces. Think about places that create momentum for you. Think of places you think more clearly and feel better in. We can't create plans that stick from places that remind us of all the plans that haven't. We need to embrace the idea that third spaces are like trusted friends. You can rely on them. It is the reason we have parks and coffee shops. It is why we blaze trails to hike and have home offices. Third spaces are where we train our brains to see life differently and to get things done.

Have you sensed this before? Have you ever been to a place where you felt more motivated or creative? Maybe you felt more comfortable being yourself there, or there was a nice sense of community there. In my travels I have seen these spaces carried out so differently, but the same foundational idea applies. The spaces speak clearly. *You are welcome to spend time here. Stretch out and get comfortable. Use this space to get out of your routine, take care of yourself, and find a bit more of your path revealed to you.* The likelihood of meeting like-minded people who can help your plans stick is also an added benefit.

The biggest benefit to a third space is the disruption of your baseline. I have found it very difficult to try to do everything in one place. Your mind will always want to do the easiest thing possible if you do everything in one place. Third spaces allow you to mix things up.

What could be some of yours? Sort through some more memories and think of places where you have felt calm, focused, and more creative. As they come to you, write the place somewhere around the box for "third space" and connect a line to it. Take your time with it; there is no rush. Remember, if you are currently feeling stuck and you write "my bed," well, all I can say is that you know what will happen. Change comes through relationships, and that also means our relationships to the places around us. You need to start seeing your relationship to places differently, and we will need to get very deliberate with how we use our spaces.

Rinse and repeat on your poster board for every category. This will take time. Embrace the time it will take to get your thoughts and feelings out around all ten of those words. Fill the poster board with possibilities, ideas, and things you know about yourself.

The In-Between

When I told that young man I would take care of his brother (whom I knew well and already loved dearly), I didn't really know what that meant. He didn't define it for me, but the feeling I had was important. It wasn't a hollow promise. At least, I didn't want it to be. But I was nowhere near ready, not even close. When we dropped his brother off at the orphanage, I just instantly felt more connected to him. I had known this kid since he was five, I knew him well, but after that promise I just saw him differently. I saw his potential even more clearly, and I could see my role becoming stronger in his life. Still had no clue what that would look like, but I was already taking the next steps in my mind. My mind kept on flashing back to Maui and the idea I didn't need to wait to be a dad; I could start now. So, I did.

There are many, many steps between an idea and its completion, just as there are between a promise and an adoption. I needed to create some bridges from all the ideas swirling in my head toward the goal of taking care of this almost young man. I had to grab some paper and assess where I was truly at. (On a sabbatical, no permanent address, no job, just some healthy savings I had built up over the many years I worked.) If I wanted to be this kid's dad, then I had to build my first bridge toward that goal. Where to start? My mind finally realized I should define what a good dad looked like and how I wanted to show up. You'll need to do the same thing as you define your priorities and who you want to become. We aren't just putting words on paper for fun. We are redefining and becoming clear on what these things mean to us. So, I did.

Defining and Refining

A good dad supports and provides. He loves, but, more importantly, he creates opportunities. I really latched onto that idea. I loved the idea of creating opportunities for people. A dad also puts food on the table and a roof overhead, and I had no way of solidly doing that at that moment. I will tell you, when this opportunity came into my life, and I assessed my life as it stood, all of a sudden, I felt like a colossal failure. What had I done with my life? What did I have to show for it? How pathetic was I? It got kind of dark. Trust me, you will feel this as ideas begin to flow. I did feel those things deeply, but I stayed focused; I kept defining my role and hopes. I wanted new mindsets and I wanted to show up differently now that I had made this promise. My way out was to focus on the bridges

I needed to build in order to fulfill my promise. And then the fun and hard work began.

I needed a way to support my idea, a stable income to support me becoming who I wanted to be, and most importantly, I needed to continue to believe I could become this dad, this person I was dreaming up.

So, it was clear, bridge number one was me settling into a path that could support my dreams. My dream wasn't to be a millionaire overnight. Don't let your dreams grow too big too fast. Just build your first bridge. Mine was to find a stable career path.

I saw on my poster board, by the box titled "service," the word "mentoring." I saw one of my third spaces was my humanitarian work. I saw written down that one of my priorities was helping people find change and opportunity. One of my routines was checking in on a lot of the young people I had mentored over the years. A pattern started emerging. I needed a bridge to a career that would support my ideas and this little family I was creating. I wondered if I could turn my mentoring into a career. I wondered if I could still combine my humanitarian work with my mentoring. I started to see a bridge form in my mind. I could become a coach and I could charge for my service. It was a good idea, and though I was uncomfortable with it, I didn't dismiss it. There was so much more to being a dad besides having a stable career.

Quick(er) Exercise

Can you see similar patterns on your poster board? That is why we did it all on a big piece of poster board. So, so much easier for you to see patterns, connect the dots, and begin to build bridges between ideas and concepts. Those lines I asked you to draw between ideas are potential bridges to create.

Look around your poster board. Is there a particular concept on there that really resonates? Maybe you put down working with your hands. Maybe you put down listening.

What other things did you write down under the other categories that relate? Is anything becoming clearer? If you like working with your hands, value being outdoors and in nature, and being independent, those are all strong, complementary factor in your new plans. Remember, we are doing all this to make your plans stick better. Plans stick when they have backup, wing people.

So, what patterns are you seeing? Does it feel like a stronger you is emerging? We aren't trying to solve everything with this exercise; we are just trying to see what patterns are there and what ideas spark from seeing them. Simply write on the poster board, or in the margins, that idea, thought, or pattern you see. Let it percolate.

From Idea to Bridge

Another bridge was built on that paper. I saw some of my hobbies and routines and asked myself if those helped me be a good human. A job didn't just fall into my lap after thinking about it, so I started to build bridges to more existential concepts of who I wanted to become, be.

It became very clear to me that I could do this through my hobbies, my routines, my habits. Where should I dedicate my time while bridges are built? What will you do with your time as you get creative with your life and create new plans? Will you do the same things that got you stuck in the first place? Will the old ways we got our dopamine take the reins again and get us stuck again? Can you prioritize different third spaces and healthier mindsets to help you build your first bridge? That is the hope here, dear reader. That is my intention with all this.

There is an important gap between who you are now and who you want to become. We can get lost in that gap. We can quickly return to the safety of our baseline. We can give up because our plans weren't authentic to who we are. That is where hobbies, routines, and habits come into play. We build ourselves up through them as we look for opportunities. You get a chance to become something new, different, better, while our opportunities begin to show themselves.

In other words, we are buying time for more authenticity, but we are also developing ourselves holistically. Life is much more than a job or what we do; in the end, who we are matters most.

Hobbies

Hobbies are a way to find out who we are. It is exploration without the pressure. It is a chance to be curious and practice things consistently. On that poster board, I'm curious as to what you'll put down. Some may say it's crazy, but there is a direct correlation between career success and your hobbies. Think about it. What we love and what we are passionate about will ultimately guide our career choices, who we might date, friends we might have. Your hobbies also create a hell of a narrative for you in job interviews, or when applying to an internship. You don't have to be the most interesting person in the room, but we do need to be interested in life.

I will be honest. I used to put so much pressure around my hobbies. My brain and cognitive distortions would tell me that if I couldn't be excellent at something, I shouldn't try it. That mindset made me bounce around from hobby to hobby. I am not proud of it, but when I became aware of it, I was left with an important question to answer.

What do I want to do for myself?

That can also be posed as, what am I passionate about for no other reason than pure joy, love, or excitement? What do I get lost in for hours? Those were hard questions for me to ask myself. As I looked around my garage, I saw surfboards, snowboards, cameras, camping equipment—the list goes on. But I never really mastered one of them. My mindset on my hobbies was a problem.

Do you have some ideas for some new hobbies that create momentum for you and your story?

Do you feel it is impossible to even think of hobbies? I hear you. Don't give up on this process. At times in life, it is hard to imagine things not being hard or impossible. You are not alone with those thoughts. I'm hoping you've seen a glimmer or two of hope. Things can be different. Accepting that is a good enough start.

I need to be a bit blunt, too. If your current hobbies don't create momentum for you, then they aren't really hobbies. They are distractions, and we don't need more distractions in this process. We need authenticity. Your hobbies are a guide to your authentic self. Explore. Be curious, but don't obsess. A piece of advice really changed my view on hobbies: Go 80 percent of the way, so it stays fun. The other 20 percent takes too much effort, unless your goal is to be an Olympic gold medalist. Be aware of that 80/20 rule, as they call it. Perfectionism will ruin your hobbies, and in turn your plans.

The Volunteer Stretch

When I was a teen, my parents signed me up to volunteer with the Special Olympics. I remember it was so early on a Saturday and it was uncomfortable. I was dropped off for a few hours to assist the athletes in training for their events. Communication was at times difficult; following directions or maintaining the athlete's attention was next to impossible. I was drowning and I wanted to quit.

Then I saw a little bit of progress and a smile from the athlete I was working with. The bond was set and, for a moment, I began to see beyond myself and my uncomfortable feelings. My thoughts of quitting went away and, maybe for the first time (I hope not), I got beyond myself and all of life's drama. Something shifted, and I think I really saw the value of service, of volunteering. I know you will, too. I want you to explore possible avenues to serve, to give back to your community, as a way to get beyond your head and life and into the shoes or issues of another or a community. It will do you more than good. In serving with the Special

Olympics, I found my strengths. I found a deep well of patience in me. I found a desire to get a smile out of someone, and I learned to care more about someone else's success, not just my own. Like clockwork, my life improved, and yours will too.

Stop, Research, Sign Up

That wasn't just a nice story. Volunteering is the secret sauce if you feel stuck, if things feel off, or just bland. Volunteer. There are plenty of ways to volunteer.

Consider:

- Working with animals
- Working with underprivileged adults and children
- Helping the environment
- Helping educationally
- Visiting the elderly

Many times, I hear, "I'm just not ready for school or a job." The structure might make you nervous; interacting with others might make you nervous. A good bridge to a job or a big step in your plans could be volunteering. Should be. The pressure is less, but the ability to build your skills is still there. I have seen huge progress with people I mentor after just a few weeks of volunteering.

So, open a web browser and search for volunteer positions based on your interests and zip code. Look over their websites and make a commitment. Try it a few times, not just once. Give it a chance to chip away at your old mindsets and expose you to new ideas about yourself.

Volunteering/Hobbies Expose Priorities

I don't envy you. The amount of mind-numbing distractions there are in this world is overwhelming. You will face every trick in the book your brain and your feelings can throw at you. *Just a little more scrolling on the socials please (!), an early wake-up? No!!!!, being uncomfortable, yeah right!* I've come to understand that most colleges and even high schools value service on resumes, especially consistent service, because the story it tells is profound: this person gets it, this person can stop time, almost, and bring themselves to see others and their community deliberately and consistently. I want this for you, especially if you feel stuck right now. Serve until you feel what I did—that incredible moment when you don't matter as much—and watch the more negative mindsets melt away.

Hobbies and service expose our priorities, which is beautiful. I saw this correlation early in life and I created a program around it. For years, I took rowdy, shut-down teenagers all around the world in hopes they'd get to know their priorities a bit better. Like I said, it worked beautifully.

I took travel and made it therapeutic and different.

On a particular trip in Swaziland, I saw that magic change a really cool kid's life. For a while he had been stuck, not progressing. We had already spent a good chunk of time doing some manual labor, mentoring some awesome kids, and seeing the beautiful country. On this day, we were in the bush, far from any city, volunteering at a school. We were clearing the land and planting a huge garden so that there would be crops for the school. Most kids only got one meal a day, and a lot of the time it came from school. It was a harsh reality for all of us. We worked hard, and toward the end of our time at the school, I was approached by this kid. He wanted to talk, and I was happy to do so. We found a huge rock in the sun, and we climbed up on it and he started talking to me.

I really liked this kid but, that day, I respected the hell out of him. He started timidly, but then he opened up. For the first time, he told me things he had never told anyone. I appreciated his trust. I listened as it just spilled out of him. It was beautiful. I don't know how long we were there on that rock, but I could see the group was done. I didn't care. They could wait. This kid wasn't done. When I felt it was appropriate, I asked my first question: What cracked the dam? He simply said, "I saw what these kids were facing on the daily and it gave me courage to deal with what I needed to face in my life." We hugged, said we would talk later, and climbed off the big rock.

It probably feels impossible to find your priorities when you feel lost. I'm not minimizing what you have gone through or what is in front of you. I'm asking you to connect with yourself through hobbies and service so you can find clarity on your priorities. We will need these as we make plans that stick. They will become filters through which we will pass opportunities and ideas. When you know your priorities, you won't take a job or set a goal unless it aligns well with you.

Priorities form identities and, unfortunately, all of us have been creating identities by over-identifying with our fears, anxieties, and feelings for too long. An identity, whether positive or negative, is a long-term investment, meaning it is built over time, and we normally expect our investments to compound, meaning they take a life of their own and grow. I hope that all that assessing we did earlier has exposed you to what you have been over-identifying with. Don't worry, this creation process we are in will help you identify different and more positive priorities. Prioritize this process and you'll feel hope.

The process of creating is fluid. That is why I have you work on poster board, with a lot of room to expand and figure things out.

I have given a few suggestions for bridges to get you unstuck. Third spaces are incredible opportunities to break your mind free from the routine. Service and hobbies are bridges that create momentum. Just like the proverbial snowball, you'll gain speed.

But what if the gap between where I am now and where I want to be is just ginormous? What if everyone around me just wants me to get a job and move out? What if all we feel is pressure to perform or change? Who has time for hobbies and service anyway? You may feel others have different priorities and there's no way yours will win out. All that, and what I am saying is true. This is life, and it can feel overwhelming. Rents need to be paid; food needs to be on the table. But you matter and your meaning matters. Let me explain.

I lived in Spain for a long while. I love Spain. Please go; it gets passed over too often when people visit Europe. I was young, brash, and a bit idiotic when I lived in Spain. I didn't have a lot of real-world experience, yet being young makes you really sure of yourself and how you see the world. But Spain got under my skin; it changed me. I was luckily there long enough for the country to give me another perspective, another possible way of living.

I remember I got called out one day. "Josh," they said, "you live to work; we work to live." Time stopped again for me. Whether it was my brain translating the lesson from Spanish to English, it took it a moment to sink in. I'll let it sink in for you now too.

A goal is just a goal; possibly, work can be just work, a bridge to a better you, if you want it to. I think a lot of times our mindsets get overly focused on the end goal and the work it takes to get there, instead of the process of becoming that occurs by deliberately practicing.

Goals

I needed to bring all that up so we could understand goals better. In the process of creation, you will need guideposts—a roadmap—and goals can serve as those. You need goals, but maybe not as you have previously set them.

If there is a ton of pressure on you just to get going, to get a job, to take a class, whatever, those feel like goals or action items that measure our progress (pressure!) and inevitably our worth (what if I fail?). They are not, because they aren't permanent. They are bridges, too. You cross over bridges and soon, past goals are in the distance. But if you see goals as bridges to get you going, to get you to where you want to go, your priorities defined and in action, then the pressure is off, and I can't tell you how empowering this perspective is. The end goal, all that pressure, isn't just for you to get a job and get out of the house; the end goal is for you to become what you prioritize. My hope is that you are tracking. Don't get lost in the weeds of the goal and its inherent work; instead, get lost in the idea that this is you building your life, and your life will contain many goals/bridges.

A Personal Priority, a Goal, a Bridge

I started a business a while back. It would take a while to develop. I realized early it was only going to cost me money. I had a ton of concerns. I had also just started the adoption process with the boys (boys? Yes, one turned into two quickly).

Message from my past and current fears: *I am just bleeding money and not making much, money is scarce.*

Remember, when I started the adoption process, I had no clue what I wanted to do with my life. I just knew what my priorities were. I still hadn't established myself fully.

So, while being interviewed to manage the produce area of a local grocery store, the lady interviewing me just had to ask. "Josh, why are you applying for this job? Your resume and skills are way beyond this." I was honest and direct. I needed a bridge. There was a gap between where I was and where I wanted to be, and I thought this would help. They offered me the job right on the spot. I checked my ego, my pride, and I built a bridge. You are going to need a lot of bridges and ego checks. Don't be afraid of them, because the life you prioritize is beyond those bridges. Build them, even if they feel forced upon you by others. They aren't the end goal; they connect you to your future you, they'll get you unstuck if you let them.

That conversation in Spain about work changed the way I looked at goals as well. Goals, especially at New Year's, feel like work, but they aren't. They are your priorities turned into metrics. Goals are needed and very necessary for life only because they help you track your progress. If we can make this shift, then we don't have to see our goal as the enemy or something to easily drop. You'll want the information your goals give you, and that is a huge shift.

How to Set a Goal

1. Settle on a priority.

2. Where does that priority want you to go?

3. Do you agree with the direction?

4. Solidify the big picture (Priority: move out with friends. This priority is moving me toward saving to move in with friends. To do so, I need a better job!)

5. Check in with yourself and your mindsets ("But I don't know if I have the skills for higher pay, or the confidence").

6. Identify needs: more money, more confidence, more skills.

7. A goal is forming: "I want to move out by summer."

8. Assess/introspect: is there a hobby, volunteer opportunity, or task that can help me build confidence and my skills while I work toward my goal?

9. Start there, build bridges—there were a lot of little goals to get you to your big goal.

10. Put in the work.

Rinse and repeat and keep stretching yourself. Feeling more confident? Look for a job, then build on that. Feeling like it is taking too long? Assess. Can you push yourself harder now? Work two jobs!

Remember, goals are data; they'll keep pointing you forward while giving you feedback. Don't personalize your goals, meaning be offended by them. Just see them as clear starts and finishes. Goals are honest friends. No one will tell you how it is quite like a goal.

Have confidence in your short-term goals. Believe in yourself. Follow through. Create consistency. Build your self-worth. Value your personal integrity. Goals will teach you all this.

Goals are great. They will chart your progress. Your priorities should inspire your goals and keep that spark of motivation alive. Third spaces will mix things up and add some new energy and hope, but your confidence, your confidence is key.

I know of only one way to build confidence.

Playing Dress-Up

A while back, while working at a school for at-risk teens, I ran into a challenging young man. I loved him, but he was a handful. He was endlessly entertaining and was hyper-focused on his past life and all things drugs. It was one of those situations where you instantly knew what this kid was all about the moment you looked at him. In this case, it was overbearing. Any time I meet someone who's all about one thing, I know their priorities aren't straight. It was the case with this kid, too. Something needed to change. I was close to him, and I did have his trust. Intervention after intervention failed, and we were getting nowhere. There was nothing strong enough to get him to want to change.

Something changed after an amazing chat in the rain in India. After laps and laps around buildings and gardens talking about life and soaking in the hot Indian monsoon, I realized something unique about this kid. He was so committed to his lifestyle, his mindset, and his love of drugs, that it had to count for something. I think the whole time he was at the school, we all saw it as a negative. Still, it occurred to me on that hot and rainy Indian night that all I had to do was help him build a bridge toward other priorities, and I thought of a crazy idea to get him building different priorities. It was simple, maybe even stupid, but it worked. I told him when we got back from what turned out to be an epic trip that we were going to the local thrift store. That's all the information I gave him.

This section on creation revolves around your openness to thinking differently, and what I hope evolves from it, as well as routines. All that we have discussed builds to this point. Our routines are our deliberate practice. They will give huge dopamine hits and fuzzy nice senses of accomplishment. They will bring you hope, and that's all we really need in this world.

Routines rely on your word. When you say you are going to do something, you do it. No excuses, no questions asked. It is incredibly personal because we are the ones who shut off the alarm. We act and live and make decisions mostly when no one is looking, but that is when it counts the most. You do what you say you are going to do, even when no one is looking. Routines bank on this. They fail when they can't.

The only way third spaces become a thing in your life is if you go. Going to a coffee shop and having a good think about your life, coming up with some priorities and some bridges to build, only works if you actually go to that coffee shop and have a good think. Priorities are focused and bridges are built if you bring some paper and pen, and you stick with it. Goals are formulated and tracked from there. You get the point. If you don't believe yourself when you say you will show up differently in this world, then it is truly a nonstarter.

And that is where I was with this kid. So, after getting over the jet lag, we ran over to the local thrift store. We bought slacks, button-up shirts, ties, belts, nice shoes, and a briefcase. I asked him simply to start dressing up every morning. To shave, shower, and put on a tie, and don't forget his briefcase. That was his new backpack. I didn't ask him to drop drugs or to never talk about them again; I just asked him to dress up for life every morning, that's all, and he hated the idea. I couldn't force him, but I asked him to believe me. He wanted other things for his life. I know deep down inside he didn't want life to end up always with him in a complicated situation based on some choice he or the drugs made.

My goal with all this was for him to finally believe in himself. Routine would be our friend in the process, and I knew that, after a while, each and every time he put on that tie, he would believe in himself a little bit more. Believing would become routine. He could trust that he could follow through, and confidence would be a natural result. So, the experiment began.

Believe Yourself

As you sit in front of that piece of poster board, I would like you to think about some routines that you can build that will make you start to believe yourself more—not believe in yourself, but believe yourself.

Many start by making their bed every day; others may wash their face daily. Small, small things. But they all serve the same purpose: they build momentum for you. And remember, momentum is nothing more than confidence.

So, as you jot down ideas for ideal routines, start small and simple and have that story in your mind. Every day, this kid put on that tie, and every day he followed through, he had an excellent day at the school. He thought differently and saw things differently. Yes, my idea was also to make him stop dressing like a deadhead and bring a bit of formality and ritual to his life. He started talking differently and thinking differently. New, fresh ideas started showing up, and they were fun to explore.

I want that for you as well. We will talk building routines in Do, but I needed to frame them not as items on your calendar or to-do lists, but as fundamental beliefs in yourself.

Your routines will naturally become habitual. Habits are like the blood running in your veins: you know it's there; it runs its course and carries out its job daily, often without any interference from you. That is why they are called habits. Your habits are the same, so it is imperative your hobbies, routines, goals, priorities, and third spaces build healthy and cherished habits. Cherish probably seems like a silly word, but it is purposeful. Our love of coffee and hitting the gym become habitual; so do gaming and porn. You can trace any negative habit back and see how our goals, priorities, hobbies, etc., all contributed to the creation of that habit. This process I am taking you through can build a good or a bad life. Truth is truth, no matter how we use it.

Cherish your habits. Jot away on that big piece of poster board what habits come from your priorities and the goals they will create. If you want a job, or if you want to head back to school, or just feel better, not so trapped or stuck, well, think of what habits you want to be known for.

Your routines will build them.

Your previous mindsets will fight you every step of the way, so I need those present for you as well. When you write Mindsets and draw that box around them, I want you to be incredibly honest with yourself. Your mindsets will impact your ability to create, and if we don't create something inspiring, authentic, and real, those plans won't stick. We just won't do anything; they'll be fun ideas only.

After I made that promise to take care of that dying young man's brother, I didn't realize how much power my mindsets had, and how deceptively clever and entrenched they were. When that young man passed away, I got started on the process of making good on that promise. I had clear priorities now, but I was thirty-four, and my life consisted of habits built from years of routines, goals, bridges built and crossed, and mindsets. I underestimated my mindsets.

Underestimating Our Mindsets

To get you caught up fast, I told Carlos (my oldest son now) about the promise I made to his brother, and I asked him and another kid (Ivan) at the orphanage if they wanted to be a part of my tribe, only this time, we'd call it a family—and I said that I would move heaven and earth to fight for them and help them make a life for themselves. I didn't take it lightly, even though it seemed dramatic. But you gotta realize that this was a huge change for me. I was a nomad, an entrepreneur; once I graduated from college, I never worked for anyone and answered only to myself. But all of a sudden, I was asking two kids if they wanted to be part of a family I wanted to create. I was probably a bit insane. Big risk equals bigger reward, am I right?

I'm right, but more on that later. I got the ball rolling. I had no stable housing, only entrepreneurial jobs, all that stuff I mentioned. I was at the ground floor, maybe where you are right now, and I was daydreaming a lot. Cooking up what could actually be. Which was good, but my mindsets brought me crashing down.

As I was making plans on my own big piece of poster board, I started to doubt myself and my priorities. I remembered failing at football, or when I let down this or that person, especially Supergirl. My habits at the time were screaming at me; they were telling me that nothing I currently did habitually meant I could be a good dad.

My fear of letting people down and my long list of failed relationships told me I was not good with anything long-term. My mindsets, built through habitual thoughts and feelings, were pouncing all over my poster board, yelling and screaming that none of it was possible.

That kid I had dressed up like a little midtown Manhattan lawyer faced the same thing. Our mindsets will come calling and crashing down on us, no matter how inspiring our plans are. This is not a negative; this is a good sign that we are on the path to positive change. Any time you are up against some friction, it is your brain, your baseline, and all the messages that add up to our collective mindsets. In the Assess part of this book, I tried to help you get to know them, and now that knowledge will help you catch on as quickly as you possibly can when they come kicking and screaming.

Know them intimately, write them down. We need to make some plans around them now, and we need to get creative. Remember, there is always the other side of the coin to counteract these mindsets.

Do you feel you know your personal mindsets now? If not, my hope is that these stories and concepts will lead you to consider them and understand what is true about them and you.

I grew up on a rollercoaster. I'm sure we all did. I didn't notice my scarcity mindset until the Great Recession. After scrambling to save my parent's businesses, my scarcity mindset began to grow in the shadows, and it began to eat at my appetite for risk and erode my entrepreneurial spirit. I counted on that risky, entrepreneurial side of me most of my life. Then I decided to adopt two boys and, suddenly, things felt scarce, too risky, and impossible. I ran numbers, pored over my finances and my current situation, and my mind screamed: "You are an idiot! Why did you make that promise? You got those kids' hopes up. You are a horrible person." And so it is with us. Momentum lost, mindsets win out, when we let them.

It was humbling to go into that grocery store and get a job watching over bananas and oranges, but I dressed up for it and nailed the interview. My mind, its set messages, and my ego were all screaming at me post-interview while I walked back to the car I'd borrowed from my brother-in-law to get to the interview. Literally, as I was hitting unlock on the key fob, I received a call. It was a project that paid incredibly well, and I took it. I walked back into the grocery store and explained to the lady I couldn't take the job, and I finally got it.

I got what it really means to want to do whatever you can to make things happen, even when things feel scarce and lost—when you think you can't even get close to meeting the moment. I felt that with those boys. I had no clue how to make it work, but I didn't want to feel scarce anymore, especially with my relationships. I was going to commit to those boys, and I knew it would build a bridge to other, greater things for me and my ability to forge strong and healthy long-term relationships.

I know this story feels a little fairy-tale-like. It was. I literally had the store's apron in my hand as I walked to the car. I committed to my priorities fully. I had to get started, so I did. And life gave me a gift. That project was a huge burst of short-term confidence. The momentum from it is still felt today.

I didn't need to be a millionaire to try. I just had to believe in myself and start building bridges. Walking into that interview was me saying to myself, not the world, that life wasn't scarce, and that I was willing to start at the bottom until I could find my next opportunity. I was telling myself I valued momentum over pride and ego. And I got lucky because that project landed me others, and as I built my relationship with those two boys, I built my life back up and retrained my brain—thank you neuroplasticity—from a scarce one to a more abundant one.

That one project didn't make me a millionaire, not even close. I moved in with family, I borrowed cars, and I relied on the goodness of others as I traveled back and forth from Mexico, building my bond with those two boys. I cashed in a lot of chips with people I had helped over the years, and I saw the great abundance in life. More importantly, I started to become a dad, to think like a dad.

Which brings us to the end point of this section on creation.

All these concepts, the priorities, the little goals, and the sturdy bridges we build, the routines and habits turn us into someone, and I hope you like who you see on that big, analog piece of poster board. I hope all the ideas and self-awareness scream at you from the board and fill you with thoughts of abundance and success.

Plans become.

You become.

Becoming is what we should call living.

I hope you see nothing but authenticity and hope on that board. If things aren't adding up, if they don't seem real to you at your core, well, I hope there is more room on that board, or you can go grab another and start over. I want you to see you all over that board, the good, the tough, and the possibilities. And what could get in the way. That is self-awareness. That is you on that board.

Creating my family has not been a fairy tale come true. Life isn't that way. It is a rollercoaster, and nothing about it is fair.

Please let me hit one unintended consequence of you deciding to make plans that stick—of you deciding to engage in life again, whether it's beaten you up a bit or we've just been scared to live it. It is a peek behind the curtain, it is a glimpse that life is abundant and good if we decide to engage in it.

The other side of my scarcity coin was abundance. I am not just talking about money here. Up until the day I made that promise, I had lived an almost otherworldly life. I traveled the world. I created projects that helped tens of thousands. I filled my storage unit with art and incredible finds from all over the world, hoping one day to build a home. That promise shifted me from nomad to homesteader, and I had no clue what I was doing. No clue.

I want to highlight something I have come to understand as another Capital-T truth. People are good. They want to help. No matter how badly we've been hurt by other scared and scarred humans, there is still goodness out there. I have been hurt badly as a kid. I'll save that for another book, but my scarcity mindset initially made me distrust people for a long time. Even while success piled up around me, I didn't trust people; I relied on myself and myself alone. And I was alone. And all of a sudden, I was on another path. I would never have taken back my promise to those boys and, trust me, that commitment has been tried and tested in many amazing and difficult ways. But I was never going to be alone again. And you might think that's a good thing, but for that thirty-four-year-old nomad, that was scary as hell.

Going back to school after a semester off, or believing you can pass classes you previously failed, is similar. Your new priorities and the bridges you are building through goals, routines, and habits will bring you exactly to the point where I was—scared but hopeful.

I didn't forget that I put mentors on that list. My commitment meant I had to live life differently, and we can't live life without interacting with people. Your plans will need help, support, guidance, and cheerleading.

I want you to write "Mentors" and draw that box around it. If you are feeling creative, draw a big heart around it. I want you to start listing all the people you can rely on. Even if there's one person by that box, or even if you can't think of a single person, don't worry, they will come. People are good and we believe in your plans.

If I'd only known about the amazing people who would come into my life after I made that promise to myself to do differently in Maui, or after the promise I made to Carlos's brother, maybe it would have been easier to take certain risks. I am forecasting this for you because I wish I'd known about it. I will be more honest: I did. I still didn't trust people. Trust me that people will show up once you put these plans into action, and these people will be your mentors, whether you call them that out loud or not. They will teach you constantly, and sometimes it is easy and fun and, other times, a mentor will come into your life, and it will be hard. I see everyone as mentors now, as teachers, and they don't necessarily know it. It makes me feel more abundant, maybe because I am more in control.

Seek out mentors and people to support your plans, and if you scrape your knee or bruise an elbow while doing it, you've learned, and you can be grateful to those experiences and people.

People are good, your plans are shaping up. It was fun exploring and creating with you. Now it is time to do.

Recovery Lifeboat

While I was planning out the outline of this book, I had to contend with a few things. One is my severe ADHD. Another was that there are plenty of books that talk about planning, goals, and habits, really good ones. I didn't want to reinvent that wheel. But I did want to meet you where you are.

I have more than 10,000 hours of coaching and mentoring. In all those hours, I realized that most of the discussion around how to set goals or create a habit is intuitive. I have seen over and over people take flight quickly once they improve their mindsets. After hours and hours of picking apart memories and mindsets, I'd get an ecstatic call: *I landed the promotion! I volunteered today! I met my savings goal; I can get that car!* It wasn't ever about not knowing how to set a goal; it was all about what was getting in the way.

You will have setbacks, and many of them will feel incredibly unfair. Some of them we can learn from because they were errors or misjudgments we made. Others are unfair, blindsiding, and out of our control. They feel like failures, and they hurt.

I am often asked, "How do you recover when it all goes to complete shit?"

I have no intention to portray my life as rosy and perfect. To be honest, my second son has been one of my greatest teachers in this life. I have never felt the depth of failure or pain like I have with him. Yet, I still try. I still love him dearly, unconditionally.

I realized early on that there was a process I could go through to help me through this pain, this insecurity, these perceived failures. It includes many of the concepts we've gone over. Here is the recipe:

1. I had to let myself feel it completely, not in my room in the dark, but in a safe place. A third space. There was a particular hike I did whenever I was in it with my feelings and my youngest son. I would hike and feel. Whatever came out came out, no holding back. I wasn't curled up in a ball crying on the hiking trail; if I needed to, I would have been, but my mind knew I could find relief on that hiking trail. I gave my brain that consistency. This could be a song, a trusted friend, a nice warm cup of tea and comfy chair as well.

2. I didn't try to solve things right away. Just don't. Feel it completely.

3. Time for sure helped.

4. After some time, I went to my brainstorming third space, and I journaled and assessed. Much as we did in Part 1. I drew

lessons, understood what mindsets were at play, and generally just allowed myself to write it all out.

5. I still didn't solve it.

6. I looked for connections, just like we did, when we assessed you and your mindsets. Patterns would usually appear, and I wrote them down.

7. Then I would allow myself to try one new thing to get me back on track toward my priorities, a small goal, one I was pretty sure I would get a win with.

8. I would then get back on the horse.

9. Ride on toward that sense of accomplishment.

10. Hope felt restored.

At this very moment, I am in a trusted third space, writing. Simultaneously I'm in one of the biggest struggles ever with my youngest son. I am in the thick of it. Still feeling it. I am not rushing to solve it. That is just us trying to squash our feelings. I'm feeling like I want to cry and write this book. Once again, we are these walking contradictions, and it is absolutely beautiful.

I'll head on a hike here soon, and I'll probably watch that epic live performance of "Silver Springs" by Fleetwood Mac; no song or performance makes me feel like that one. Talk about creating beauty from conflict and broken hopes and plans.

Your plans will stick, my friends. They will. Just get back on the horse if things get hard.

Part III

DO

It Is All Simple, Don't Complicate It

It seems like I have the same conversation at least once a week. I usually expect a few phone calls into any mentoring or consulting relationship I am creating—and these calls usually come with a specific kind of expectation: anticipation for transformative, radical advice. I don't know how to describe it, but I will try. It's this energy that gets created when a person wants to change. It is this feeling that the suggestions for things to practice and do need to be sexier, bigger, crazier. (Damn hyper-novelty and social media!) It does feel as if I have let the person down when I explain the simple fixes I want them to get started with. I have them acknowledge why it feels this way. Simple is less sexy, but it's much more vulnerable. The smallest changes are often the hardest to implement. We don't need to complicate things by going big and announcing it to the world. If you want your plans to stick, then go inward for a bit, stay focused, and keep your plans under your hat while you build the initial momentum you need. This all happens before we bring others into the equation. It's too much pressure and too much dopamine to announce plans before we've created the right amount of momentum. So yes, I know, I am not giving us a lot to brag about on social media, but that is not the point of any of this. I am here to make your plans stick.

Filling the Inevitable Void

Whenever we decide to make a change, we are replacing one thing that isn't working out so well for another that we hope will work better. This creates a void, or a vacuum that gets created during the process of change. We will need to be aware of it, and we will need to fill this void with new, positive things, or it will fill automatically again with old habits and patterns.

This is just another thing to be aware of as we implement our new plans. That void will need to be filled, and it is our responsibility to care for that process. These new goals, habits, and routines we are creating should do the trick; just stay aware of this and on top of what you are filling the void with.

Which isn't easy to do on your own. So, instead of making big announcements, find some people you trust.

Mentors/Accountability, Again

You will need help.

I have struggled my whole life with the idea that I need help, support, or assistance. It's a common struggle for many. Plenty of attention has been paid to and books have been written on our human need for vulnerability and support.

I still struggle with it, though. Not with the concept, necessarily—it is important as we are making new plans based on our previous brainstorming that we start to include right away those mentors and people who can help us get to where we want to go. But I still sometimes grapple with my understanding of their role in this process. And how to create this support system.

We all have outlets and places where we can cultivate relationships that can help us foster our growth and lend us the support we need. They are all around.

Where?

Well, what do you spend time on? And where do you invest that precious thing we call time? What third spaces did you come up with in our big poster board brainstorm? These are places where we can develop relationships of support.

A young man I was working with was struggling to get going. He was motivated, but he needed support and accountability. He lived alone in a big city. He didn't have a car or a ton of money. We had worked hard to get him a job, and he had some bigger goals he needed to save for. It did feel like the deck was stacked against him. He spoke to me about one of his favorite third spaces. It was a gaming cafe. It was always full, and it didn't break the bank. He acknowledged that video games had been a vice in the past, but he felt he had momentum and perspective, and could gauge well if he was slipping back into endless gaming. I appreciated his awareness and honesty.

So, I simply asked him, "Anyone cool at the cafe?"

"What do you mean?"

"I mean, does anyone seem cool there, like that you talk with, have other common interests with, or maybe they just really kick ass at a game you like?"

"Yeah, Johnny."

"I want you to make Johnny your mentor or accountability buddy." He started to speak, but I cut him off. "Johnny's a good guy, right?"

He laughed, confirmed he was, and confessed that turning Johnny into a mentor felt nerdy. I told him he was already nerdy. He laughed but shot back, saying it just felt weird.

I asked him if he felt he needed to formally invite him to be his mentor. He admitted it felt that way. I laughed. I got it. Yes, there are times when that might work, but when seeking support, you are looking for good people who you can observe more, look up to, and seek advice from, no matter if it seems basic. We observe our mentors. We notice what they do; that's a huge piece of this. But we also seek their opinions, advice, and feedback, and that doesn't have to be terribly, crazy formal. It could be a simple decision to look at someone differently. It is mostly on you—to be more deliberate with that person and to care and listen. And then, apply and see if the observations and advice create goodness and momentum for you. Rinse and repeat. Your boss, an elderly lady at church, an extended family member you call to catch up with every so often—mentor is a title bestowed on someone by you, mainly in your head, because of a decision you made to practice that relationship more deliberately. It works vice versa as well. As you spend time in third spaces and places worthy of investing your time, people might notice potential and take you under their wing. They observe you as well over time, think they can help, and start to make little investments of time, advice, and listening.

The magic comes from your consistency, which people will notice. It doesn't happen on day one. But it results from investing in yourself and your plans and staying consistent with them. That, as we are trying to do here, should be your number one goal: be consistent.

Look out then for mentors and people around you who inspire, even if from afar, or through the written page, or on the internet—that's a start. My grandparents, who have all passed, continue to mentor me every day. How? I sit and think about what they'd do in certain situations and try to emulate it. Mentors really do come in all forms.

You can, with time, make any relationship much more formal by sharing your goals and asking them to keep up with you and see how your goals are coming along. At first, you may need to follow up with them as they follow up with you, and they may need to see that you are serious, but most will own the relationship you are setting up if you take those steps to make it more formal.

Johnny became a consistent and funny mentor for my client. He just called him out in a way my client could relate to and, all of a sudden, my client was more social and had a partner—a major goal of his. Johnny was just a mirror for my client to see himself and his progress. Johnny helped immensely to help my client find different solutions to whatever was getting in the way of his plans.

That's the magic of a mentor.

Key Decision

Before we really jump into these skills and tools, we have a key decision to make.

Creating the initial momentum falls on you, and that, especially when we are feeling stuck, can feel impossible or even laughable. I need you to know that I recognize that. As fun as all this brainstorming is, it will require you to get things going. The inspiration and excitement from creating plans dissipate quickly as our brain craves and pushes for your baseline. You are in a battle. You are the general, the army, and the medic. In the beginning, you will be wearing a lot of hats.

The ten words we listed when brainstorming new plans were purposeful and important. They are our guideposts now in this section.

So, let's learn how to Do—to do even when we don't want to, when the gravitational pull of our bed, computer, or phone is so strong, it feels impossible. Let's start with creating some strong scaffolding around you doing things.

Headstrong

We get too stuck in our heads. We get too reliant on things, technology, and people to solve, fix, or do things for us. We've become too dependent upon our brains alone, our dishwashers and washing machines, our phones and Wi-Fi. We forget just how powerful our bodies are, especially when it comes to creating momentum for ourselves.

I get tons of phone calls in the middle of the night. I have the uncanny ability to sound perfectly awake even though I was pulled from a dead sleep. I get a good laugh when the callers ask if I was awake. (Who knew that could be a skill or talent!) Most of these people call me because they are desperate, panicking, or feeling so low they just need some way out, some relief. I appreciate the trust and never take it lightly.

I have a formula for when I get these calls.

I listen.

I seek to understand.

Then I get them into their bodies.

Honestly, it works so well. When the mind is in control, we don't know what thought, feeling, or emotion it will grasp onto tightly and not let go. The mind's tenacity can take us down some dark and scary roads and make us feel incredibly stuck and hopeless. I am so grateful when people call, because I know they felt some momentary hope when they picked up the phone.

I won't lie; I get tons of resistance when I transition from being very understanding and validating to creating a different type of momentum through action and getting them into their bodies.

In less stressful situations, I would ask you to do a little cognitive restructuring, which is the simple skill of choosing a thought or fear that creates stress and anxiety and replacing it with a less stressful, or calming, one. Remember my formula using adult perspective and evidence-based thinking? It is a version of that. In the moments late at night, when your brain is locked, it can work to do some breathing and body work as well.

Sun Salutations & Box Breathing: Two Routines for Positive Change

These simple tools allow you to get out of your head and into your body so you can do some thought replacement or look for some adult perspective and evidence to calm the messaging you are getting from your brain.

Box Breathing

Think of a box. It has four sides. You breathe in for four seconds, hold for four seconds, exhale for four seconds, then hold again for four seconds,

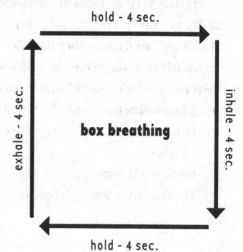

and repeat the box. Do this to help your brain release its grip so you can have more clarity of mind.

Sun salutations are harder to write about, so I have included a simple diagram. It is yoga, which is incredible for calming the mind and getting you into your body. I can't recommend yoga more highly. But these ten poses, done as a flow, create peace and are very helpful in getting your brain to release its grip.

But sometimes, on those calls late at night, I need something more substantial. I suggest that they do twenty-five push-ups, or turn the shower on cold and jump in, when the resistance is high. I have to spend a good chunk of time convincing the caller to do that one, but holy moly, it works.

But when they do, when they become stronger than their brains, when the brain's chokehold releases and they get down and give me twenty and I hear them exerting, counting, breathing heavily, and then completing the task, I get inspired because they are taking control back from their brains. When they get back on the phone, I can usually tell the difference right away.

I always then quickly ask questions about what is really going on. You can do the same through journaling or meditation. The brain has no hold momentarily; the vulnerability and power of the body is in control. I always experience my best conversations and planning of next steps in these moments. Take advantage of the break your body will give you from your brain.

I'm confident you will be able to find some clearer next steps when you give your body a chance to clear the air.

This is also why regular exercise, no matter what that looks like for you, is so important.

If an exercise routine didn't make it onto the poster board earlier, consider it, please. I'm not talking about marathons or hiking Mt. Everest tomorrow. Some stretching or a walk will get you started and help you build strength and confidence.

Let me summarize this simply now.

We must exert, move, act if we want to get unstuck, and we can't do that through thinking about it. We need to trust and rely on our bodies to get us unstuck. They will show up for us the best they are able if we don't let our minds talk us out of it, especially with thoughts that destroy our confidence and positive feelings for what it means to have our bodies.

There's a label for when the brain just gets stuck analyzing; it's called analysis paralysis. It is simple to understand: your brain is trying to solve everything within the confines of your head. We all know that is not possible. Change requires action and testing the waters. Taking a risk on an idea or thought. Be aware of how your brain gets paralyzed.

Your brain will also throw perfectionism and anxiety your way as you begin to actually do things. Why start if you can't guarantee you'll do it well, and what if you fail and everyone is there to see? Our brains are so smart and tricky.

Our biggest antidote to analysis paralysis and our brain's tricks of perfectionism and anxiety is to always start small. If a daily task or a goal you are setting for yourself sets your brain off, then you need to break it down into smaller chunks.

Small, baby steps: getting out of bed, making your bed, brushing your teeth. When we are stuck, truly stuck, then we get some wins by starting off incredibly small. Don't judge yourself here; just try.

The Habit of Indecisiveness

After we got back from the first trip to the orphanage—remember the story that got this whole thing started?—I got a crazy lung infection from surfing in some pretty gross water while on the trip. After I recovered, talks began around the next trip, and all I could think about was what went wrong on the first one. So many things went wrong. I became paralyzed by needing to know whether everything would repeat if we decided to go again. What if someone got arrested again? What if people got sick from the food? Luckily, I had good friends who calmed me down eventually. Each of my worries and fears had another side to the coin. I could learn the lesson from whatever was overlooked or went wrong and find another way to go about it. I remind you of this because, when talking with people about why they give up on their plans, I usually find out it wasn't something catastrophic. It was analysis paralysis—not being able to control the unknown, with a little bit of perfectionism thrown in. They gave up before they even tried.

So, if you feel your brain is too much in control, let your body get to work so you can get clearer on your next steps. If not, we become incredibly indecisive, and that soon becomes a habit.

Our Roadmap

What we will be doing here now is learning how to put scaffolding and structure around the brain. We will do that in five steps.

1. **Starts and Finishes**

    We will work on your ability to create an action item and define its start and its clear finish.

2. **Building Routines**

    We will build routines based on what you value and consider your priorities.

3. **Creating Feedback Loops**

    We will discuss ways for you to get feedback, so you know you are making progress.

4. **More Concepts to Consider**

    We will make sure you are set up to face the demanding world and not give in to negative concepts and mindsets.

5. **Your New Best Friends Who Already Are Best Friends: Patience and Curiosity**

    And lastly, we will remind you not to rush it—all this takes time— and to stay curious.

    So, if you are feeling stuck, if you can't even think about taking what we did in Create and this book, then we start with a focus on you building your body over your mind.

Starts and Finishes

This simple tool is incredibly powerful; don't just say *duh*, please. In our battle to control our minds so we can follow through, we need to be clear; we need to give our brains clear starts and finishes. Everything we do and plan must be planned through this lens. All that brainstorming will become overwhelming and impossible to convert into plans unless we break things into manageable chunks. Telling our brains to just go get a job won't work; watch as your brain sabotages those plans. From now on, we don't plan open-ended tasks, at least at the beginning. Accept this.

I need to give you one other tool before we jump into the details of starts and finishes.

I have my own version of AI. It's not an app and, as always, it is decidedly analog. I call it Josh's AI, because that is the limit of my creativity. This tool will help you break down your plans into more manageable chunks. It helps you get a better sense of the lay of the land.

Josh's AI

Unfortunately, most don't give much thought to their plans. We are reactive—mainly to our brains and our current situations—not proactive, like we were during Create, when we were able to brainstorm without judgment.

We mostly feel on our back foot, or on defense, because we're being reactive to thoughts or to the moment. We lose confidence and slip more into the fears and power of our brains and nervous systems.

Becoming proactive means we learn to anticipate and then set intentions around our actions.

Anticipate.

Intention.

Old-school AI.

When I teach this skill, I go about it in a real-world way. I have the person I am working with give me an example of an event coming up that is giving them pause, or a ton of anxiety. This is usually pretty easy; our brains are always chewing on something. We discuss it in detail. The conversation is always about the what-ifs of the event or situation. The cognitive distortion of negative filtering is strong at work. After listening and validating, I will then simply ask, "What can we really anticipate about this event or situation?" Silence. Thought. Brain releases its grip.

I will then hear some very real concerns, very true things to be anxious about. The concrete, not the feelings or the emotions around the event or situation.

I have them repeat back what they can honestly anticipate. They usually become even clearer.

- I anticipate that I usually get nervous before tests.

- I fear I haven't prepared enough.

- What if I go blank in my interview?

- What if no college accepts me?

If they were worried about a test, or getting that job, or getting into that college, I would then have them anticipate what they could actually control to counteract their initial anticipation.

- I can get organized around what I need to study.

- I can make flashcards or find videos that help explain the subject.

- I can read over my notes.

or

- I can review my resume and job listing.

- I can practice describing how my experience relates to the job listing.

- I can do a mock interview with a friend.

or

- I can get some help on my essays.
- I can do a lot of self-care while I am waiting to hear back.
- I can boost my volunteering now, so my resume looks better.

All of these were great ideas and anticipations of what they could do to control the situation.

I let it sink in. Anticipation around things we can control calms the nerves and keeps the mind from locking on to uncontrollable things.

After a minute, I remind them that they just got really clear on the source of their anxieties and fears. The brain wasn't able to control the situation anymore because we breathed in some clarity, perspective, and new ideas. They can feel a release in their body because clarity brings hope and peace. Then the conversation turns, and we begin to focus on our intentions.

Intentions to me are like goals, but mainly they are structure and scaffolding for the mind. We turn those anticipations into actual measurable goals.

- I will sit down and organize myself for this upcoming test this afternoon at four.
- Tonight, I will make some flashcards.
- I will set an appointment this week to meet with my college counselor.
- I will spend thirty minutes looking over the website of the company where I will be interviewing to understand their product and company culture better.

When the mind strays from your anticipations and intentions and into a more anxious or fearful state, then the hope is that it bumps up against your intention. With time and practice, you can get it back on track and not chase after it for hours. You do so by grounding yourself again in what you anticipate and intend to do.

So, if we are stuck on the idea that we can't work a job, that working with customers would be too much, that you'll never be able to run the cash register or get out of bed on time—well, honestly, those are things we need to anticipate but take back control of. They are valid concerns, but they aren't as insurmountable as your brain would have you think.

If you anticipate that your anxiety about working with customers will lead to failure at the workplace, you have identified a need, you have anticipated some work that will need to be done. And we can work with that.

To further our explanation, if working with people or jobs with customer interaction feels like too much, our intention then is to get better at that so we can succeed. We are clear now. It isn't just an overwhelming feeling or thought. You clearly anticipated something, and now we are clear on what we want too. Our need for a job, our anticipated fears, and our intention to get better at it is a roadmap for us to follow.

Take some time to identify a sticky situation in your life right now. Think it through, try to get to the truth or reality of the situation, clearly state what you anticipate about it all, and then take a moment to get clear on an intention around what you anticipate you'll need to be successful in that situation. Now let's learn how to use this skill of identifying our needs and wants and turning them into plans.

My AI formula is a simple way to identify needs and wants beyond your fears and anxieties.

But we are now back to building that structure and scaffolding for your brain.

We need to take those clear anticipations (needs) and intentions (wants) and give your brain some next steps, some clear starts and finishes. In fact, I will be bold here again: you shouldn't attempt or do anything, especially in the stuck state, if you can't identify the start and finish of what you are attempting.

This is ultimate deliberateness. You can't do anything on a whim anymore; that is too risky. We need wins, and the way we build toward wins is to deliberately convert our brainstorming in the Create section into plans we can do, ones where we can see where we start and where we finish. Without a clear starting point and a finish line, you will see your brain and its bag of tricks get to work faster than anything you've ever seen. It will throw every excuse, anxiety, or fear your way in hopes that something will stick, and you will give up.

If I sit down at my computer to write or work without anticipating where I am at or how I am feeling, if I decide to get to work without that knowledge or intention, I will find myself on YouTube in no time. Laugh along with me; we know it is true.

But if I am clear: *Josh, brain, I am going to write on these topics for my upcoming book*, or *You need to finish this assignment for this consulting project*, or whatever it is, I'm able to review where I am at with this thing, how it feels, what's the lay of the land. I try to get really clear on where I am starting. This might look different for you, but we aren't dissimilar at all. I struggle with motivation and letting my brain get too far ahead of itself. You are in process, not perfect. Me too.

Once we get the lay of the land for where we are starting, we can set the finish line.

I want a job. I need to put some applications in. I'm starting from scratch today. That is where you are starting from, that is reality. So where do you end? Saying you are going to apply to twenty jobs in a day is your brain's way of setting you up for a loss. Well, it's eleven in the morning, I got up a bit late, I know I will get hungry in about two hours. Before I start job applications, I'm going to get into my body somehow; I'll go for a walk, take a shower, shave, or get my makeup on. All bodily activities. So, I guess I have about an hour and a half for job applications. This is still too open-ended. Focus. Turn that hour and a half into an intention to complete five solid job applications. You now have the lay of the land and clear finish before lunch. Rinse and repeat after lunch. Get into your body, get the lay of the land. Maybe you are feeling lazier post-lunch. What can you do to combat laziness? Another walk, a run, some yoga? Get your body moving, then set another clear finish line. Set yourself a reward at each finish line if needed. Feel the sense of accomplishment at every finish line fully, but don't let yourself think the race is over. Starts and finishes are you breaking down big goals and intentions into small chunks and getting some good dopamine along the way.

This brings us to building routines. Routines are built by every small start and finish you accomplish. Rome wasn't built in a day. Give yourself the grace but not the excuse. Build yourself over time, and don't bite off more than you can chew. We want to work in reality, not in our fantasies of how things could be.

Building Better Routines

Routines are your priorities in action. It is important to give space to them, to breathe and play out, maybe even to play around a bit and have fun.

Our priorities need to be clear, and the hope is here that during Create they became clearer. You should have an idea of the life you want to create. If you feel unclear, then go back to that big piece of poster board and see what becomes clear. What patterns are there? What through lines can you see? Let's ground the next few steps in our priorities.

Perfect Day

There is an exercise I would like to teach you. It is called Perfect Day. When we were brainstorming on that poster board, we put down a lot of ideals and hopes. How would you convert that into a day you could live out fully?

What time would you wake up?

What would you do next to help you create momentum for the day?

What self-care would you include?

What nonnegotiable activities would you plan for your day? Exercise? Social time? Time for you to explore creative ideas in a coffee shop?

How would you fill a whole day?

See the example I give.

There are a lot of hours in a day. Challenge yourself to fill them with meaningful things. Take all you can from your poster board and translate those ideas into activities.

Then, I want you to live that day. If you have work or other responsibilities, that is great. That helps you anchor your day and build off the momentum. You go from getting a haircut, to going to the gym, to getting some healthy groceries, to visiting a friend and going for a walk. Nothing has to be fancy, just fulfilling.

Why do this?

We need the data.

Now that we have ideas of where we want our lives to go, we have to see what works, what doesn't, and most importantly what mindsets and parts of ourselves will still get in the way. We need that data.

Don't fear failing at it, just try, and get yourself some data so we can see what we are still up against.

That is why we practice a perfect day. It gets us excited, and we can try out some of our new ideas.

Quick Step-by-Step Guide to Building Routines

After we live the perfect day as best we can, we become familiar with the routines that we like and that help us. What follows is advice on how to create routines that I believe will help you stick to your goals.

Routine Creation

1. Consider what pattern you are trying to create.

Hope: I want better hygiene and confidence so I can be more social. My acne is out of control. (We've all been here!)

2. What tasks or events come from this hope and new pattern?

   - Washing my face to help clear my acne.

   - Finding better products that I like and want to use.

   - Shower daily in the morning to wake me and start my hygiene.

   - Wash sheets to help with my acne.

   - Create a better place to put dirty clothes so I know where they go.

   - Set a day to do laundry so I don't leave it until the last minute.

   - Create a better plan for organizing my clean clothes so I don't repeat clothes.

   - Keep the room clean so I can invite friends over.

These are all possible routines to build that come from your priorities, and they all have a why attached to them. As we mentioned, your why is your motivation. Your routines need a why built in, so those tasks more easily turn into routines you can live with.

3. Convert your to-do or tasks into routines:

   - Wash my face first thing when I wake up and right before bed.

   - Find a place for my hygiene products that is accessible and not easily forgotten.

- Turn off alarm, then shower immediately.

- On Sundays, I wash my sheets and my clothes.

- Dirty clothes go in the basket, always.

- Use hangers, fold shirts, fold pants.

- Pick up room for five minutes before I go to bed.

4. Practice these routines.

5. These are clear starts and finishes and are simple.

6. Assess daily what is in the way and start fresh the next day with more resolve.

These routines, over time, will create your habits. Soon, you won't even think about these things. Then you can look at your priorities again and see what tasks come from them now, create new routines to practice, and then add more positive habits to your life.

May I suggest a few routines to develop? Here we go.

1. Create a Master To-Do List, Look at It Every Day

Often our biggest demotivator is the unknown. The unknown builds and builds; it lurks and oftentimes becomes scarier or more unknown the longer we ignore it. It becomes easier to postpone and not see it than it is to confront it.

But face it we must. The easiest way to do this is to grab some more paper and create a master to-do list. In the beginning, this will be more like a massive brain dump. We need to get everything out of our heads, out of the shadows. As scary as it might sound, it is cathartic and relieving. Maybe this will be the first time you are seeing what life is requiring of you right now. That's okay. Whether we are super behind in classes or our finances are in such a mess we can't look at them without panicking, I'm here to tell you, it is okay. It is our reality right now. There will be solutions, ways forward, but we need to ground ourselves in our current realities so we can understand what to prioritize.

Categories to think about:

1. Personal life
2. Email
3. Real mail
4. Finances
5. Work
6. Family
7. Social life
8. Education/school
9. Hobbies
10. Our personal belongings

Write these categories down and start to give them each a good think. Review. Stick with it. If the house is a mess, the car needs an oil change, you have a test or a performance review coming up—think through it all and just write it down without judgment or dwelling on it. We just need it on the paper; we need to see it and to give it some air.

Take some time, don't rush; this master to-do list will turn into our daily priorities and plans.

2. Establish Your Daily Priorities

After you feel you've got it all out of your head and out of your emails, and gone through the mail and onto paper, we need to prioritize. There is no right way to do this. Some action items have due dates; some might be labeled emergencies or carry social pressures; others can wait. Take a highlighter and put an asterisk, or a few exclamation points, by pressing matters. Start to parse out what will take priority. Many ask, how do I choose? Here's the good thing: if it's on your master to-do list, it needs to be done at some point, so there is no right or wrong answer here, just action. Crossing off one item will build momentum to work on another.

3. Use Buckets

Our brains are fickle. Remember, information is power, and for us to feed right information to our brains in this process is key. Having a master to-do list is great, but that list will intimidate your brain. It is too open-ended. Not enough structure.

If getting stuff done is a problem for you, then let me suggest a few ways to help your brain calm down and get on board.

I like to look at my day as buckets.

1. I have a morning bucket.

2. An afternoon bucket.

3. An evening bucket.

4. And a resistance bucket.

The first three are easy to explain. We need to look at our days and compartmentalize them. I have come to learn myself that there are better times to do certain activities. My mornings are for the hard tasks, the things on my to-do list that require some effort and time. I like to put in my morning buckets the things I want to resist most. My brain and body are fresher and more energetic in the morning, and it is best to capitalize on that. You may not be a morning person now (and it is my hope you will get there), but even if you wake up at eleven a.m., you still have time in your morning bucket to get things done.

Afternoons for me are time for creative work or work that requires ideation, reading, and long stretches of time.

My evening bucket is for me, my hobbies, my social life, and my relationships. By this time of day, I just want to connect, and I feel that if you follow this bucket system, you'll find a similar rhythm and see its benefits. Ultimately, you will make this system your own.

When I review my upcoming day, I have to think a bit on what is going to get in my way that day. Am I tired? Is there a conflict or something weighing on my mind? Do I have a particular fear or anxiety around a specific event or action item today? If something comes up, I put it in my resistance bucket. I need to see it, anticipate it, and set an intention around it. Josh AI at work. If I don't, it lingers in the shadows and sucks the effectiveness from my day. So much of our time is spent subconsciously fighting against the resistance we feel toward a particular item on our to-do list. The actual item, like renewing a prescription or making an appointment, is only difficult due to the resistance created by the messaging from our memories and the other things we assessed earlier. Get to know what you are up against; by doing a daily resistance check-in, by writing it down, it will stick better in your self-awareness. You'll notice it quicker and can take action to find the other side of the coin to your resistance. That's what the resistance bucket is for, things for me to be aware of. I want to know what I am up against that day.

Start to transfer items from your master to-do list into those buckets. If the item is of high priority, then it needs to get into one of those buckets as soon as possible, and then figure out if there's any resistance around it.

Another helpful trick for your brain is to make sure you estimate how much time a particular item will take you. Remember, open-endedness is our enemy. Don't put four three-hour items in one bucket. But please start to understand how much time it takes you to accomplish certain daily tasks. There is no right amount of time, but if it takes you three hours to make a call to the pharmacy, then we know you are up against a lot of resistance, and we have some more digging to do.

So, a morning bucket might look like:

- Review day (five minutes)
- Breakfast (twenty minutes)
- Exercise (twenty minutes)
- Hygiene (thirty minutes)
- Head to work, school, the home office (fill in time)

Then you can add work action items that cleanly fit into the morning buckets with the time needed to do it well. Emails, meetings, or meeting prep. Time allotted. Correct order. Rinse and repeat for the other buckets.

DO   177

You may need to get super specific with your action items. Exercise or Hygiene might be too vague. Specificity is scaffolding, don't be afraid to get into the details. Your brain will stay calmer and more focused.

- Update calendar (five minutes)

- Overnight oats and a protein shake (twenty minutes)

- Yoga and the treadmill (twenty minutes)

- Shower, shave, get dressed (thirty minutes)

- Drive to work, listen to this podcast (one hour)

Specific details help build better routines and habits.

4. Set Your Schedule the Night Before

This is different from us just throwing things into buckets. At the beginning, it might be too overwhelming to assign an exact time to each of our items. Keeping them in their buckets is fine until you gain some momentum, but eventually life will require us to assign a time.

- Wake up at seven in the morning

- Look at and update calendar from 7:10-7:15 am.

Using the calendar on your phone will help you make the transition from putting things generally into a bucket to adding a set time and day. We get there with time.

I need to be bold here again. If you are doing all this planning the day of, it won't work. The resistance and your past patterns will be ready to play first thing when you wake up. If we've already reached for the phone and doomscrolled before we even got out of bed, it will be very hard to gain momentum back from our brains and their patterns from that point on.

I highly recommend always planning your day the night before. In fact, here's the boldness: I think our success rides on this habit. The morning of is too late.

At night may feel too hard. I've heard over the years that some can't sleep due to thinking about the next day and all they have to do. That is resistance at work, and it will get better. You can anticipate that and find evidence to help you soothe your resistance and worries to sleep. With effort, things improve. It will also help you create a better nightly routine, which I will get into shortly.

Planning at night is a good thing.

When you take the time, all of maybe ten to fifteen minutes, to look at your ever-evolving master to-do list and formulate a plan for the day, I promise you can almost begin to crave it. The biggest benefit, though, is purpose. You will know your purpose first thing when you wake up because your priorities and plan are already in place. No more grabbing the phone or some extra Zs. With practice, you will feel purposeful and deliberate with your time and your day, and that creates loads of meaning and momentum. That momentum and meaning will shift your perspective and outlook on life, and soon you'll start to see opportunity in things you couldn't see before. That's how this all really comes together.

5. Use Technological Help

Technology can get such a bad rap. Our mastery of it is what is important here. If it has mastery of us, then we know where we need to get to work. That is major resistance. Games, apps, and the like can add positively or negatively to our lives. It is your choice and your work to be done. Our relationship with technology can produce delusion and harm to our plans. Get right with it and be honest about it, so we can then use it for our good.

- Notes app or Google Keep: you will eventually want to convert your master to-do from paper to your phone so you can update and make changes on the fly. Some will stick to paper and pen and that is fine, just keep your master to-do list current and accessible.

- Calendar: transferring your buckets to your calendar is a huge step—setting the right reminders and color codes for things is even better.

- Reminders: getting tons of notifications on your phone can be annoying, but reminders are helpful if you find yourself on the forgetful end of the spectrum.

- Alarms: obey and actually follow your alarms, please; the minute you snooze or ignore, we are back at the bottom of the hill.

- Wellness apps: meditation apps, breathing apps, mindfulness apps are plentiful and very useful to create gaps between you and your resisting mind.

You can find your technology just like you can find your hobbies, social life, and master plan. Use it for good, wisely, and you will see the momentum right away.

6. Look Out for Opportunities

This is all real. The opportunities will present themselves. I don't want you to think they will appear from thin air. You have just done the work to make yourself aware of your priorities. You got organized. You believed in yourself when your alarm went off. You believed in yourself when you set on paper all that we created and your master to-do list. You believed the evidence you came up with when you got overwhelmed or down.

Opportunities will come; I truly believe they have always been there and coming your way. We just couldn't see them, or our brains didn't want the change. We've learned the process now and, by doing so, we have invited ourselves to start seeing what is actually around us.

Remember, you were able to see the opportunities because your plans helped you get back into the world around you, not holed up and stuck.

How can I best look out for these opportunities?

How to Journal

Journaling is the best way to keep your priorities top of mind and for you to see and process opportunities. Many don't journal because it feels cumbersome. Each page doesn't have to start with *Dear Diary* and be filled with writing. I reserve that for special occasions.

Try this formula:

1 page

1 line

1 thought

I have found this to be incredibly helpful to establish my journaling practice. It got it to stick.

Briefly explained, you will only write one page. You don't write continuous lines. You write one line down at a time. That line is one thought you've been thinking. Maybe it is a concern, maybe it is a cool experience you had. By condensing our writing to one line at a time, we strip away the excess and we access the bare minimum. We give our brain structure to get us in touch with what we are thinking and feeling. Try it. It works. It almost becomes poetic: each well-formed thought leads to another and leads us inevitably to some action we need to take or an avenue we need to pursue. All of which are new opportunities for us.

LINE BY LINE

- NO DEAR DIARY HERE PLEASE

- WHAT HAS BEEN ON YOUR MIND?

- TRY TO CONDENSE TO ONE LINE

- WHERE DOES THE LAST LINE LEAD YOUR MIND TO NEXT?

- GO DEEPER

- LINE AFTER LINE

- YOU'LL NOTICE, THE PAGE IS COMING TO AN END!

- WHERE DOES ALL THIS LEAD YOU?

- IS A NEXT STEP CLEAR?

- IS THERE A PART OF YOU SEE BETTER?

- LINE BY LINE

- NO FLUFF

- JUST YOU, PAIRED DOWN, NO DRAMA

7. Create Feedback Loops

Goals to me are feedback loops. I set a goal and then I can see if my efforts are making any headway. Goals have taught me to look for evidence and find my guideposts. When making plans that really stick, you are going to need feedback loops. These can take on different forms, but you'll need to get good at finding evidence that you are progressing, or you'll give up.

Some feedback loops are immediate. Say you've prioritized your studies, you set the goal to get an A on a certain test. You drew a line, but then you failed. Looking back, you realized where you went wrong. You took study time lightly, made excuses for not reviewing, you missed a study group.

That is an example of a feedback loop. You set a goal or input something into your life, you wanted that A. You got a D. More input, more information. You processed that information compared to the goal you set. You looked for evidence or for the reason behind that D. You got it. You processed it. You understand where you went wrong so the next time around, your goal and your process will be different.

A D stings. Normally we will ignore those feelings and thoughts, but you have to send it through the feedback loop. People can help you process too. I always find a listening ear to help me if I feel stuck. Without feedback loops and the process we just went through, we get more and more stuck, because our brains are unwilling to compute the data. Don't ignore the data, take the feedback.

Feedback Loop Formula:

take time weekly to review priorities
and the goals your priorities create +

assess wins and losses as you worked toward
those priorities and goals +

journal, succinctly, on the why's behind the win or the loss +

assess mindsets present +

brainstorm new approach if needed =

informative feedback loop

Courtesy of the author

8. Be Anti-Permissiveness

I often think about the harder left turn my life would have taken if my coach had just let me quit toward the end of the season without any intervention. If he'd just written me off. I have so many great memories doing other things I was good at—basketball, volleyball, water sports, etc. I don't know if they would have happened if I had quit. Maybe football just wasn't for me, or I wasn't strong enough to stick with it. I don't know the answer to that question, but I'm deeply grateful to my coach.

Actually, I'm grateful to so many who sent me in better directions, who weren't permissive. Who in a way forbade me to give up. Who pushed me to try harder and to not sell myself short.

A while back, I was on the beach with a dear friend. We were watching the waves and discussing a project we were working on. The waves were huge, too big for me, but we enjoyed the beauty and power of the ocean as we sat, talked, and watched some amazing homegrown surfers do their magic. There was this woman, maybe around my age (late thirties), yellow board, black-and-white bikini, surfing and having a blast. She wasn't using a leash, so when her board crashed to shore, I'd grab it for her and send her back out. As I went to grab her board, one of those many times, flopping around in the waves, she asked me what time it was. I told her and she smiled; there was still a bit more light and time for her to enjoy what seemed like an epic day for the well-trained. My friend and I enjoyed our conversation some more when we saw and heard a bunch of commotion in the water. We ran to see and saw some people dragging someone to shore. We ran to help. It was her, the rad, smiley surfer woman, who was now unconscious. We began CPR. We worked and worked. Medics came, a helicopter came, but her light was gone. I felt we lost her.

My friend was amazing that day. She comforted and helped this woman's friends and bystanders; we all did what we could in the way we could, but in the end, it wasn't in the stars to save her. I got home that night and checked the local news constantly, hoping to find out she had maybe survived.

It was a rough moment. It was also a moment when I wished I had a fellow surfer friend at my side. I stopped really surfing that day. Of course, I would teach my kids, but I would just push them in the waves, or show them how things were done in the shallow, smaller waves. I mainly found myself watching them surf, vigilantly, from the shore. The ocean can be a scary place, and I guess I just found myself trying to mitigate the risks for everyone. But I still loved being in the water. I wasn't a crazy pro surfer but the water was a great place to be for me, a strong third space. Whether paddleboarding, surfing, scuba, or sailing, I loved being on the ocean, and it all just stopped that day. I didn't trust myself in the ocean much anymore, though I never really said that out loud.

When I was even younger, on the way home from a movie at the mall with my mother, a lady and her daughter ran a red light and t-boned the car I was in. The impact hit my door and fender. My dad rushed over immediately from home while the police sorted through things, and I just hung out in the minivan while I replayed the accident over and over. When I got home, I swore off driving in cars ever again. Just like I did later with surfing. Only that time, with my parents, I screamed and cried.

Unbeknownst to me, my dad heard what I was saying about the accident to my sisters and immediately knew he had to do something. He wasn't going to be permissive. He came in and started filling my head with visions of yummy desserts. I immediately wanted all the things he was describing. There was a catch, of course. We didn't have any of it in the house. A car ride was needed. I refused, half-heartedly, but finally gave in. I was in the car that very night, getting dessert, and my fears and promises to never ride in a car again were gone.

Like I said, I wish I had that surfer friend near me at the time of that tragedy who would have done the same thing for me. I didn't at the time, and I gave up for a while on a really good thing for me.

As you build your routines, schedules, feedback loops, etc., I hope you will also consider the people around you and how they will help you make your plans stick. Do you have friends who make excuses for you? Do you have people around you who, like frogs in a boiling pot of water, will drag you back down because they don't have any plans for themselves or their lives? Don't let people be permissive with you or your plans. Find people who are striving for goodness and new horizons. Surround yourself with people who won't let you back down from your plans.

Positive & Negative Communities

Do your current communities uphold and support your priorities? If they don't, change is needed. This does not have to be dramatic. It may include a break-up, I don't know, but if the people around you aren't supportive, then we set clear boundaries and, just like finding a mentor, we find new communities through our hobbies and third spaces. But back to boundaries.

This concept has become too black and white, and I've become concerned over time, as I have coached, that most draw these super harsh and dramatic boundaries. Of course, don't surround yourself with people who bring you down. But this is life, and those people are unavoidable; they can even be in your own family and friend groups. Yes, you aren't obligated to anyone, and there are situations where strong boundaries are necessary, but whenever we have had to set a boundary that will help us move forward or away from a more toxic situation, let's not make it about the person; let's make it about our priorities.

When someone asks me, "Why you aren't coming by anymore?" or says, "You are no fun anymore," I never say, "Well, it's because you are a real drag and a complete waste of my time." No, that creates more negativity. No, boundaries are just a declaration and focus on your priorities and by doing so, hopefully you inspire others to change, not create more drama.

Personal Integrity

As we discussed earlier, part of this—I would dare say the foundation of this—is your personal integrity. When you say you are going to do something, you do it, even when there aren't people around you to support your plans and not let you give up on them. The foundation starts with you, but please surround yourself with good, anti-permissive people, starting with you: don't be permissive with yourself.

A couple years back I was in Lake Powell; we were on a houseboat with some work colleagues. I joined at the last minute. I love Lake Powell. I spent time there over a few summers as a kid and fell quickly in love with the sheer rock walls, the endless sunny days, and just being with my friends as we skied, wake boarded, and built bonfires at night.

When I arrived, I quickly realized that wake surfing was a big thing now and everyone was just so stoked to get out on the boat and wake to enjoy. I immediately tensed up. I hadn't surfed for a good couple of years by that point and all my perfectionism, wanting to be cool, all that stuff, just surged up in me. I told everyone I would for sure go out, but memories flooded in from my football days and high school. I didn't want to not be good at it in front of all these new work colleagues.

The group was a rad bunch of people. I shared a little bit of my fears with one of them, a cool guy who just looked at me like my coach had years before, like my dad had, and said simply, "We are going out now." The surfer friend I had needed all those years back had arrived.

We went out on the boat. I watched someone give it a go a few times, then this guy threw me a life vest and told me to get out there. I was out of shape and in my head. I jumped off the boat, grabbed the board, and tried to get myself in position. I was in Struggle City, trying to figure out how I was ever going to stand up on that board. They could see I was struggling from the boat. I was out of breath and wanting to give up. I almost did, until the thought came to me that I had done this before. It was different, but I was still good on a board. I yelled out to the boat that I was going to try to stand up in a way that made sense to me. The way they taught wasn't working for me. They all gave me a thumbs-up. I positioned myself, gave the nod, and the boat roared to life. In a split second I was up, on my feet, feeling the board again, understanding the wake and the power behind it. I also had a huge smile on my face, and so did my friend. I rode the wake, carved it for a while, and then I fell off when I got too cocky. I fell back in love with the water that day, and I felt a huge shift in me that I'm still building from today.

I know this book has been teaching you how to set good plans into motion. This book has also dealt more with what is getting in the way: the inner you. I have tried to have you see things anew, to get and feel creative again after being stuck for so long.

You know you have to be at the center of this. No one will do it for you. As you look at your priorities, as you formulate those into goals and habits created by your daily routines, the first steps have to be on you. Just reading this book is a huge step. I applaud you. I applaud you just like I patted myself on the back that night on Lake Powell. I overcame something. I was pushed by the people around me and myself to find my way out of a certain fear or hard place. I almost gave up. In my mind, in the water, I thought, "Let me just bail a couple of times and call it good. My pride and ego will be bruised, but I'll manage." I was so glad I wasn't permissive with myself. You'll be proud of yourself too.

Be anti-permissive.

9. Starts and Finishes Recap

When things are left open-ended, we suffer. Our brains love familiarity, and the unknown and impermanence of life are often way too much for our brains.

When I got into that accident, my dad quickly put a definitive finish on what could have become an open-ended fear. Most of us watch movies and read books to their conclusions; don't leave a scene or part of your plan unfinished.

When you attempt a thing, no matter how small, understand where you are starting, know where it ends. Know when it feels good to start and when it is right to finish. Completed tasks will pile up in your done pile when you plan this way. If something makes it onto your schedule, know the end. Anticipate and intend. But know the end too.

Don't give your brains the reins. Hold those reins lightly, guide your amazing brain toward the destination you've set, and stick with it, be ready to pivot and to make plans around your plans. Your brain will just want to think about your plans or what could go wrong. Start knowing your end in mind.

Most of our plans don't stick because we don't understand the place from where we are starting and we have no clue where we are going, how it will end.

Loading the dishwasher has a clear starting point and ending point.

So does putting in a job application.

So does working on an overwhelming fear, one little bit at time, one small chunk at a time, one clear and deliberate start and finish. This is exposure therapy.

You wanting your plans to stick is a good start, but how will your efforts accomplish those plans in the next hour, the next day, or week? It has been said to start with the end in mind. That's great, but do that in small chunks, getting the dopamine and sense of accomplishment from each finish. Remember to look back at where you started from. That is how we will build. Checking the foundation we are building from all these small steps. That is how we will find our own version of success. Believe that.

P.S.

A start and finish you need to consider is your sleep schedule. Having control over this is probably the most important routine you can establish here. A wonky and varied sleep schedule can wreak havoc on your priorities and daily plans. I acknowledge that we may face some severe uphill battles here, but creating the healthiest sleep schedule for ourselves is important work. If professional help or outside consultation is needed, please, make those appointments, make this a clear priority.

Part of this is knowing what you need to sleep well.

How do you like the lighting? The temperature? How much sleep do you need? Do you have comfy sleepwear, bedding, etc.?

Last point of emphasis: we tend to sleep more when we haven't addressed the mindsets and anxieties that burden us. We tend to avoid the day when we don't make plans the night before, as we've discussed.

Getting your sleep schedule on track is of high, high priority.

Courtesy of the author

10. Set Your Morning and Night Routines

As we grow into our priorities and the plans that come from them, it is easy to see how much of our adult lives is not in our control. Our studies, our jobs, relationships, you name it. It can all feel very uneasy, which then makes it all easier to avoid.

On that first trip back to Africa, when I went searching for projects, I didn't account for how bad the jet lag would be. For the two-plus weeks I was there, I was up like clockwork at three or four a.m. Wide awake, not even the least bit tired. I had hours to burn before everyone got up and before my adult responsibilities came calling. I loved it. I was twenty-six at the time, still young, and very careless with my time. In those early hours I found a groove, a nice routine. I would wake up, sneak to the kitchen, and make a hot cup of rooibos tea. I would bundle up and make a little fire in the fireplace. I would read a bit from the book I had brought. It was still dark, but I made it a point to do a little exercise, enjoy a piping-hot shower before other guests used all the hot water, then I got ready to watch the sun rise over the most incredible valley landscape imaginable. I brought my journal, and I would write until the lovely cooks who made us breakfast rang the come-eat bell. I felt so in charge of my day, so settled, grounded, peaceful. I had tons of energy and clarity. I held the reins: life didn't feel so out of control; it didn't demand everything of me without giving anything back. On that trip, the importance of a personal morning routine where I could practice things for me solidified. I have had different versions of my morning routine over the years, but I find them to be the antidote for feeling out of control. The minute you put plans into play, you'll feel vulnerable, out of control. Expect it.

I realized soon after that the importance of a night routine, even though it took up much less time—planning my next day, hygiene, another cup of tea, and a nice chapter in a book. I took time, dialed in my sleeping arrangements, and made sure my sleeping schedule was in good form. For you, this might be a huge deal. Varying your sleep time, when you go to bed and when you wake up, can really work against your plans. Consider the control you'd feel by just getting your sleep schedule under control and waking up knowing what you wanted the day to bring. Consider just taking a little bit of time in the morning to invest in yourself and that little extra time at night to unwind and stay in control by looking ahead while sipping a nice cup of tea. Your version will differ from mine, but the concept is tried and true.

If you feel that scheduling life, whether into buckets, or down to the hour, is too much, begin with some clear starts and finishes of a morning and evening routine determined by you and for you. You'll believe yourself more as you invest in yourself more and follow through.

I'll trust you to know what's healthy for you. Grabbing your phone in the morning and checking the news might seem like a good idea, but I would urge you to consider more simple and inward-focused activities as you build trust in yourself and your priorities.

These routines are a way to practice kindness toward yourself when your mind or the world might feel quite negative. This is where I'd love you to start if you are feeling beyond stuck.

This is how we practice self-care.

Morning Suggestions

- Make your bed
- Attend to your hygiene
- Journal

- Exercise
- Eat a healthy breakfast
- Review your day

Evening Suggestions

- Put your phone away
- Plan the next day
- Reflect

- Attend to your hygiene
- Get to bed early

Add to your liking from here!

11. Let Go of Busyness and Hurry

Our society feels that busyness somehow equals success. If you are always rushed and important, you must be important. Not true.

Being in a hurry, or always looking busy, is us putting on a show. It is not a balanced life. It leaves no room for introspection and assessment. It is fake. I should know. It pains me to say it, but if you were to phone ten of my friends and ask them why they don't ever reach out to hang out, they'd say, "Josh is always busy." But that isn't true. I make time for people, always, but somewhere along the line I bought into the BS that busy means important, and people noticed.

I'm working hard at changing people's minds about how busy I really am.

I hope, more than anyone, that my boys have seen a positive change here.

Our plans aren't meant to make us busy and in a hurry; they are meant to create a meaningful life.

Courtesy of the author

12. Be Patient and Curious

I have an addiction to cars. Always had. I've been known to buy a muscle car immediately after watching a *Fast and Furious* movie. I've gone to bed, exhausted, maybe a little depressed, only to realize in the morning that I've won a truck in an online auction. It is something I have had to work on. I still love cars, and that love can get me in trouble to this day.

I've gone to buy many a car sight unseen. I'd fly in and drive it home a thousand miles. The last car I did that with had over 200,000 miles on it. My friends think I am insane. I am.

We've been throwing around a lot of concepts in this part of the book.

- Priorities
- Goals
- Habits
- Routines

- Master to-do lists
- Feedback loops
- Anti-permissiveness
- Starts and finishes

It may feel overwhelming. Remember, small chunks. There is a way to ease into all this and still build yourself momentum.

I was about halfway home in that truck with 200,000 miles on it, crossing the desolate Nevada desert. when a friend called me out of the blue. I told him what I was doing, and he laughed and told me I was crazy. He asked, "Aren't you worried about breaking down out there?"

The thought had crossed my mind more than a few times. But over the years of my crazy car buying, I've learned I need to test the cars I buy. I need to see what they've got. I don't mean beating them into the ground the minute I get in to drive. There's a patience and curiosity to the process I've come to learn and love.

I turn that anxiety into curiosity. I foster a sort of patience with the car. I look around the engine, check the fluids, belts, and hoses, read gauges, and smell my way around the car. I check in with the car and listen for any weird noises. I'm patient with it as I drive it along a hot desert highway. If something goes wrong, I feel capable enough to deal with it. And so, the miles pass.

When I bought that old VW van I used so often on our trips to Mexico, I flew to my cousin's wedding and then hopped in that unknown van and drove eight hundred miles back to school in Utah. I broke down outside of Vegas. The same happened in an old Jeep my family had. I learned not to take things personally. Things break, I break, plans fail, and I have had endless hard days. I have to have the patience and curiosity to track down the problem and find a solution, whether it's a broken car or a faulty step toward my goals.

When we brainstormed in the Create section, I hope you felt some hope, some excitement, some curiosity about whether those ideas and thoughts could be turned into plans. This section was a way for you to test those ideas. To kick their tires, so to speak. Don't be afraid to test your ideas and your hopes. You are more capable than you realize. If you run out of gas or a tire gets a nail, well, that's part of the story, part of your process. You'll manage just fine if you don't personalize. If you can see the adventure in your plans, then they will stick.

Patience and curiosity will be your trusted companions on this journey as you stumble through your priorities. As you see goals come and go. As your routines ebb and flow until you get it just right for your current situation.

Be kind to yourself, but realize that laid out for you in this section was a whole list of things for you to try, fail at, then hone and try again.

Mile after mile, that's life: you check the gauges (assess), fill up on gas (create), get an oil change (do and pivot), and head out on another adventure (become). The only thing that is on you is to start the car, to get these concepts moving in your life. Don't be afraid to test yourself. Adventure awaits you.

Be patient and curious as you get your plans to stick better.

Part IV

BE

It has become clear to me that we are most asked about, and most often judged by, what we do. Our actions are most visible to people. Our job titles and accolades seem to interest people most. I believe this to be a flaw and technique used by most all of us to avoid truly being vulnerable with those around us. Imagine our conversations if we told stories to one another about what it is actually like to be *you*, to exist in your world, and what *you* are doing to improve, become, or learn more deeply. I'm not sure we could handle conversations like that. It would expose too much for each one of us. It would make us focus more, hopefully, on the things that matter most.

But that is what we are going to be doing in this section. I am going to simply share a story and offer you what I learned, and maybe an opinion or two.

Start by Being Vulnerable through Story

I want you to be able to do this too. We've learned through stories together. You've learned to own your personal story. So how do you learn to be vulnerable and share your story, your insights, and who you are becoming with others?

There is always a choice in all this.

It is a choice to share our stories. To let people in on our stories. Remember, I didn't want to share other people's stories and insights in this book and then teach and preach. I just shared my stories of my struggles to make my plans stick.

My friends make fun of me a lot. We will go to dinner or have a bonfire and we will all be sharing stories.

I know you do this already. Sharing stories is natural.

Inevitably, when I am sharing a story of mine, my friends laugh and roll their eyes.

They call it being Brazier-ed. I have experienced a lot of diverse and fascinating things. I, just like you, want to share. My stories can at times be over the top. But I need to share my stories too. Why?

Because our lessons become complete when we share our stories.

Our stories, life, all the lessons become real when we share. So, if you really want to make all this learning we've done real, share it. Tell stories. Mess up telling those stories. Laugh when telling your stories, especially the hard ones. By doing so, people will tell their stories too, and you'll learn even more, and that's how we will all grow together.

My friends might make fun of me, but I know they all appreciate everyone's stories, no matter how grand or small. The appreciation is in the sharing.

Risk a bit and share a failure with a friend. Open up and make this whole process real for you too.

See as you share that more stories start flying and soon everyone is feeling more hopeful, more possible, because no one is alone in this crazy thing we call life.

Back to Be

Getting your plans to stick means you want to improve. It means you care enough to be aware of how you are showing up in this world. You are the leader of your plans. Your plans ultimately bring you experiences and growth that should stretch and mold you into a better person.

We know this, but that is how the world changes. Individual incremental shifts. Every time you check off an item on your to-do list or finalize a plan, you become something different. You grow and oh, the waves of change this causes! All for the good.

Your being able to set your priorities and to follow through with them with plans, goals, habits, and routines is the path this book has followed, but I care even more about who you become, how you show up in this world, and the outlook on life that come from all your efforts. As you walk the path assessing your current state, as you find stronger and healthier messages, as the evidence screams that you are capable and worthy of being creative with your own life, I hope you become proud of who you are becoming. This process builds confidence. It builds trust in yourself. It makes you like yourself more and, as a result, you are no longer arrested and can feel free to take risks and create. Those precious mornings and evenings when you invest in yourself and create momentum for your days will guide your bigger plans. You trust that you will take care of yourself first, and then you'll open yourself to life and what the day brings. You become someone who invites a challenge and the hard work it takes to make our ideas and plans come to life. The only way I know to bring all this together is to paint for you some attributes and characteristics that are worthy of your thought, time, and investment. I will illustrate them through real life stories. I don't want to preach here. I just want you to give these ideas more than just a glancing look and a passing thought. I would love for you to wrestle with these concepts of what it means to be a good, effective human. My hope is that they will be woven into your planning. As you create opportunities for yourself, I truly desire that you think on these things, use them as filters—making sure that you are showing up your best in this world.

This is me Brazier-ing you. These are my stories, but I know you'll learn from them. Remember the finer details are mine, the lessons are all of ours.

If you want these things as well, your plans will stick because they will have become much more than plans, they will have become your legacy, the life you've built, over time, with tons of mistakes and solid lessons learned. You'll look back at the time when you felt so stuck, so unmotivated, or so deflated because life just felt impossible, and you'll breathe a ton of adult perspective onto those memories. You had to feel that low to learn what you have learned now, to have gotten to where you will end up very soon.

Being focused on and aware of who you are becoming will help things turn out well. It is a good thing to be preoccupied with.

So, let's dive into some characteristics or attributes that, with time and development, will get your plans to stick and grow better.

Courtesy of the author

Be Resilient

I have only really felt like a celebrity once in my life. We had a promising project growing in a small town in northeastern Brazil. It was decided that we needed to visit and get things on more solid footing. Plans were made, cheap flights booked, and after a night sleeping on a cold airport floor, we made it, and Brazil was as beautiful as promised.

We arrived at our small town without much fanfare. We met the mayor, the director of the private school where we would be sponsoring kids from a pretty bad situation to go, and then it was suggested we visit the local high school to see the difference in education (public vs private). We obliged, but weren't prepared for what was about to happen. There were four of us from the US, all college students, young and good-looking, depending on who you asked. We got to the school, we were given a tour, and toward the end of that tour, it started. In what seemed like an instant, all the students started rushing us for autographs, pictures, hugs; some even brazenly stole kisses—it was mayhem, truly chaotic. It took forever to leave and get to a lunch we had arranged with the mayor and other town officials. I have never felt so cool and so uncomfortable in my life. I don't get embarrassed too easily, but I did that day. We got in our car and, like the Beatles driving away from a concert, we had fingerprints, lipstick prints, and people throwing themselves all over the car. We drove away cautiously and dreaded the fact that we knew we had to go back there the next day to teach an English class.

We arrived at an unassuming restaurant, supposedly the nicest in town, where you loaded up your plate, weighed it, and sat down to eat. Very Brazilian. As we entered, there was a small kid by the door who asked if he could wash the car while we ate. We were being rushed in because all the celebrity mayhem had made us late. I didn't speak Portuguese well at the time, so our hosts brushed this kid off.

We got our food and started the normal pleasantries and protocols of a lunch with politicians.

But the kid stuck around outside. I watched him. I could see him try a couple of times to get up the courage to come in. He finally did. Our hosts tried to kick him out, but I asked them to translate for me what he wanted. He wanted food, he wanted to wash my car for money, he needed help. I told him to grab a plate, pile it on, and to come sit down. All the politicians were in shock, but they didn't want to offend me. I well knew the hand I held.

I am telling you: it was amazing. Gomihno sat down with a huge plate of food and had everyone else eating out of his hand. He was charming, funny, and gregarious. He made a boring lunch incredible.

After lunch, we had to leave. I gave him some Reals and thought that would be the end of it.

The next day, he showed up where we were. I had no clue how he knew where we'd be and when. The following year, when we returned, he found me within five minutes of my arrival in the town. That kid deeply worked his way into our hearts, our group, and our lives. I learned about his life, visited his home. He came with us and the other students we sponsored everywhere we went. He wanted opportunities for himself and, any chance we could, we provided it.

He was resilient. He suffered extreme poverty and situations where giving up would not have only been the easiest option but maybe the better one; from the outside, his situation was hopeless. He survived and thrived despite it all.

Learn resilience. Don't give up. If you are rejected, find another way. Act like you belong at the table with the bigwigs. Believe in yourself like Gominho believed in himself.

If it is hard, get creative, assess, then get to work.

Be a Gominho as much as you can.

Be Regulated

While assessing, we spoke a bunch about our brains, our thoughts, our emotions, our feelings—about being more in charge of what we are thinking, how those thoughts influence our mood and emotions and therefore what we feel and how we act. Even-keeled becomes a good thing to ultimately be. We don't want our emotions to be in charge of us. We don't want to automatically act on what we feel. We don't want to lend undeserved immediacy or urgency to any one of our many daily thoughts. This is good self-regulation. Often it is an over-identification with our mind, its tricks and patterns that get us into trouble. We can become very unregulated quite easily when we do so.

After two weeks with a bunch of high school boys and other volunteers, I can become quite ragged. Leading groups, staying on top of logistics, the constant pivots, the drama of a bunch of teenagers in close quarters, is exhausting. Toward the end of an amazing trip in Botswana, I let myself become dysregulated. My thoughts were running wild after catching a bunch of the boys gambling their money. Some of the projects didn't turn out as I had hoped, and I didn't know how I was going to explain that to the families and donors. I was stressed and wasn't using any of my skills to stay regulated. Instead of journaling or doing some breathing exercises, I started to identify more and more with my woes. Until I snapped. I started to identify more and more with my woes. Until I snapped.

I'm never dysregulated in public. Long ago, I had experiences in my life where I found out how ugly I could be if I let myself get dysregulated. I made a vow that I wouldn't ever go there again. But as we know, the mind is powerful and it easily goes to past patterns. So, there I was. The kid I snapped at was doing something totally mundane. It wouldn't have been a big deal to me on any other trip, or if I had been just a little better regulated. But I went off. I channeled all my frustrations and projected them onto him and the situation. He was in shock.

I caught myself once his eyes welled up with tears. I was wrong. All our previous conversations on the trip about his sensitivity to overbearing male figures, loud yelling and verbal abuse came flooding into my mind. I really messed up. The evidence of my dysregulation showed up fast and hard. Immediately, without a word more, I just grabbed him and hugged him. I started to cry as I apologized for my words and tone. I was clear. I was calm. The evidence of what was really going on soothed my ego, and I was able to let him know what actions were his and what projections were mine. He apologized for what he was doing, and I let him in on a little bit of what was going on with me. We talked it out and we were stronger for it. We both learned the lessons we needed that afternoon, but the lesson still stings for me. It shows me how quickly we can become dysregulated and how quickly we can dig ourselves into a deep, deep hole.

Being regulated, in thought and emotion, is a worthy characteristic to develop.

Be Deliberate

I'm always envious of people who seem to know exactly what they want. I find it curious how certain fears or preoccupations don't seem to bother others like they bother me. I've observed a lot of people like that over years, a lot of them students I've worked with. They all seem to have a deliberateness to them. They don't like to leave things to chance. I learned on a trip once that spontaneity and deliberateness go hand in hand.

One night in an old part of New Delhi, we had some time to burn. It was dark, but that seemed to just increase the chaos of that warm Indian night. We were eighteen people, seeing the sights, waiting on a table at a famous chicken restaurant, and this one kid wanted a more authentic experience, so he pushed for us to do something, not just wait around the restaurant. We decided to hire a bunch of bicycle rickshaw drivers to take us around the city. The plan seemed solid enough. The drivers settled on a price, we arranged where we would be dropped off, and we all loaded into different rickshaws and the drivers pedaled away. We were seeing night markets and the local mosque. People were everywhere. I kept track of the other rickshaws. Everyone was smiling and having a great time. Except that one kid.

He was in my rickshaw, and I could see he was cooking up another plan. This kid had traveled with me plenty, and he always wanted something more from any given experience. I didn't always see it as a negative, but at times it could be. I could always rely on him for a laugh and a crazy new idea and, before I could stop him, he had asked the driver if he could pedal us around a bit. The driver said no, but this kid knew what he wanted and started his magic. He saw even more adventure in our current rickshaw ride; he wanted to experience pedaling around New Delhi. I am not going to lie, I wanted to as well.

After a bit of back and forth, this kid was pedaling around New Delhi. Cars were honking, people on the streets cheering. It was quite the sight. I turned around and saw that all the rickshaws were now being piloted by my volunteers. Everyone was laughing, smiling, taking pictures—it was incredible. I even got my turn. I looked back at this kid and nodded at him, acknowledging that deliberateness inside of him that saw more from any given situation, always.

Even though we all ended up getting split up and lost, even though it got a bit tense and crazy, no one complained. We all pedaled rickshaws around New Delhi and fell even more in love with the city, with the people, and with life. All because this kid saw a more deliberate story, a more deliberate way of living life. He took a risk. He knew he had to fight for the experience he wanted and, in the end, he always ended up creating an epic experience for all eighteen of us. The drivers of rickshaws had so much fun being chauffeured around by a bunch of crazy Americans, and we all had great stories to tell when we got home.

Living a good story requires us to be deliberate, in charge, pencil in hand, willing and wanting to write the story we envision for our lives. Be bold, take action, don't fear, just be deliberate.

Courtesy of the Kaiizen Foundation

Be Consistent

You will face waves of motivation and you will feel beached and unable to progress and move forward. Your goal is not perfection, your goal is consistent movement. Progress. A little bit more each day, that's how the snowball gets going down the mountain. There is no magic bullet here: effort creates more effort, and your commitment to be consistent—even if it is messy, somewhat disorganized, or not at all efficient—is not the judgment we are trying to make here. Not even close. Remember, your perfectionism will stifle all creativity and momentum from your plans. I'd rather you consistently fail, over and over again, than not try at all. That discomfort that comes with consistency is something we should all get used to; it's just our vulnerability cloaked in more executive language.

Think of this funny story when you make decisions around consistency, especially when the monster of perfectionism wants to end your momentum. You might think it's not a story about consistency, but stick with me, it is.

There's an amazing city on the banks of the Ganges River, Varanasi. It is the spiritual mecca for many in India, and it is one of the most beautiful, chaotic, and historic cities in India. When we go, we love to stay in this guest house on the river and watch the sunrises, sunsets, and rituals play out before us.

Our first visit to this guest house was magical, and I got lucky and shared a room with a few volunteers that overlooked the river and had just an amazing view. The journey to Varanasi was a long one so, after some good food and a colorful sunset, we all settled in for some sleep. David and I started talking and got into a deep conversation about life and some of our current struggles. We were tired, but the conversation felt important to both of us, and so we continued. It got later and later, and I was feeling it—my eyes heavy with sleep. I caught myself falling asleep during the conversation and quickly jerked awake and added something to the conversation in a panic. I then fell asleep again. David would then say something and wake me up. We'd talk some more, and we were really talking about some deep and wonderfully insightful things about life, especially David's and how he felt things were going. I'd fall asleep, he'd respond with something, I'd wake up, he'd fall asleep, and then he'd wake up when I was finishing up my response. It didn't feel like very long, but David and I carried on this conversation until the sun came up. When we realized what had actually occurred, we had a good laugh. I remembered a ton from the conversation and so did David, but sometimes there were like twenty-minute naps between responses.

Before we crashed for a bit longer before breakfast, David said, "Thanks for sticking with me last night, I felt like I was able to get to some places I never thought I would. Thanks for staying with it."

It was the most imperfect and ridiculously inconsistent conversation I have ever had. But both of us stuck with it and we got somewhere—somewhere beautiful, a landscape for David's life that looked and felt different for him.

Nothing about the situation screamed, "This is an ideal situation to have this conversation," but the conversation happened, over many hours, with little naps and micro-naps in between and a whole lot of hoping for connection and wanting to show up for someone when they needed it.

Your drive and momentum will do the same for you. It will carry you on through the long and hard conversations you need to have, it will carry you to your first bridge, and then your next. Keep showing up for your momentum, consistently, and it will show up for you. It won't be like a rocket to the moon, but it will be a wonderfully scenic adventure where you'll climb hills, take naps under a tree, and then climb a mountain, all in one day. The hope is that you believe in yourself and your plans enough to want them to consistently stick; no matter how inconsistent it all may appear, goodness will come.

Be like David and me in that conversation. You can pick up and grab your momentum again, even after you've passed out for a bit. Your consistency, like our conversation, will continue and it will take you to some pretty cool places.

Be Bold (Even When You Feel Weak)

For the longest time I wanted to be a pediatric surgeon. It was a dream not entirely based in reality maybe, but I think I always knew

I wanted to be in a profession that helped people. Being a surgeon who helped kids seemed a good enough place to start.

While living in Spain long-term, I volunteered at a hospital as a translator. A ton of tourists would find themselves in trouble and hurt and they or their families often didn't speak Spanish. We'd go weekly at least to help translate conversations between doctor and patient, or doctor and family. On a few occasions, I had to translate some difficult news. Like conversations no nineteen-year-old should have to translate. I got my first taste of the medical profession, and I was already doubting my decision.

Occasionally when translating, we'd be in the room, and we'd see wounds and things of that nature. My knees would go weak (they still do), and though I never passed out or threw up, I was probably close on a few occasions.

When I returned from Spain, I had pretty much given up on my goal to be a pediatric surgeon. Everyone urged me to continue, but I couldn't stomach it, and don't think my heart could take all those difficult and emotional conversations. So, I went into advertising and never looked back.

I ended up using my college degree wisely and finding a way to still help people, but there was always a part of me that felt like I quit too early. Who knows, but at times, it still feels like regret, so I have to use my evidence-based thinking skills to build a case that I have done some good in this world. The regret usually subsides quite quickly.

But sometimes, when I see a show or a movie, and some doctor does something amazing, I feel inspired and a wee bit jealous. Maybe that could have been me. I could have been bolder, even though I was feeling so weak.

Fast forward a good few years and I found myself in the jungles of India, working on a school we were helping to build. We were having a good time. We'd just survived a long bus ride where the driver we hired was obviously drunk and it was fun (not!) firing him and having no way home. We'd deal with that problem later.

While we were working in the humid Indian sun, a volunteer grabbed me and told me there was an old man looking for some help. I hesitated because I thought he just wanted money, which was often the case. After a while doing development work, it wears on you to be seen as only an ATM.

The volunteer took me toward the old man. He was frail, wearing white, and I thought he might be a religious man or monk. He spoke no English, but one of the kids from the orphanage who was working with us helped me translate. As he was explaining to this kid, he unwrapped a dirty bandage covering his forearm. It revealed a huge wound, and that wound was obviously close to or was infected and even had maggots in it! He said he couldn't find help from professionals and couldn't afford it anyway.

My knees almost buckled when I saw the wound. I held it together as I explained to the gentlemen through this kid that we did have a first aid kit, but not a single one of us was a medical professional. I honestly didn't know what we could do for him. I will always remember the look in his eyes. He was desperate, and I do think it took a lot for him to approach us. I told the boy to grab our first aid kit and he ran intently to our supply station. The old man just stood there holding onto my arm, steadying himself, but also sending me this vibe of gratitude. It was weird and beautiful.

The first aid kit arrived and I told the kid I had no clue what to do but to clean the wound; he'd be my assistant and translator. God bless the school nurse who'd packed us an amazing first aid kit fit for an army battalion. I didn't have any internet, but I had my intuition and this cool kid at my side assuring the old man we were going to do right by him.

So, we started cleaning. It smelled bad, it looked bad, and it was hard not to yack. But somehow in this world I got a chance to try on an old dream and I decided I could do this; I could be bold, even though I felt so inadequate and weak. Maybe that sounds familiar to you and your situation.

We cleaned with care. I used the tools to remove the maggots and to look for the eggs. I removed old and dead skin and tried to get the wound into a fresh state. It had come from an errant machete swing, he told us. The old man winced in pain often and our little assistant made me so proud, soothing and helping him through the long and arduous process. Eventually, after a lot of sustained effort and asking myself a lot of questions about what a doctor would do and me constantly telling myself not to throw up, I got the wound looking clean, fresh, and in a state where we could bandage him up, give him some general antibiotics we had, and supplies to keep it clean. He left so happy. That kid and I did the whole high five, awkward hug thing. We had done a good thing and made a good team. We didn't back down even when we felt the most lost and weak.

The whole "fake it till you make it" thing isn't too far off. Boldness requires you to step into the unknown even when the results of your plans are totally unknown. You will make them happen, guessing as you go. Cleaning that wound took patience, concentration, a good dose of common sense, and the boldness to stick with it. Doing a job halfway wasn't in the cards for our little makeshift medical team we created that day. Boldness got us over the hump and then momentum took over from there. The same process will unfold for you if you let yourself be bold, brave, and hopeful that you also can do some good for your life.

And, by the way, we did hear later on the old man was doing just fine.

Be Authentic, Always

You are uniquely you, and your plans are your unique and authentic way forward. If your plans aren't based on you, what you know about yourself, ultimately what is authentic and real to you, then they won't stick. They are someone else's plans for you. We don't want that. Your full ownership here is key.

Of course, in life we have to jump through hoops, like high school, or higher education, and find our way to somehow contribute to society. You can easily make your own plans and be authentic while following some well-grooved roads. That isn't a negative. Jobs and careers can be fulfilling. You'll look back on high school with at least a bit of gratitude that you survived. Hopefully your authenticity will have room to breathe and influence your plans, so they are as sticky as possible.

Your authenticity will come into conflict with our comparison society. Being authentic while comparing yourself to others is counterproductive, but also counteracts pretty much everything we are building here.

Note how you compare yourself to others (make that list again, work the formulas set out) and make sure you haven't compromised your authenticity. I swear a whole book could be written on our comparison culture and the death of slow, authentic human development.

Chan didn't succumb to it. This volunteer was maybe overly authentic as a young teen: dreads, or the starts of dreads, tie-dyed shirts, and an endless number of bracelets on one wrist. He stood out brightly in the already colorful slum where we were working in Zambia. We were gathering data and getting needed supplies to those most in need as determined by the slum's leadership. It sounds weird but I love the slums. There is an organization, a system to most that feels quite healthy and familial, even though there are infinite issues occurring all around. There is an overarching sense of community in those I've visited all over the world.

Chan was with me that day, and we found ourselves in a small shanty with a few other volunteers. We were dropping off some supplies and asking a few census-like questions. The family was grateful; there were many gathered in such a small space; it gave me a bit of pause. We were asked by the translator if we wanted to see their daughter. We agreed, but again it struck me as odd. We all walked in and then crammed ourselves into a small room and surrounded a bed with a twenty-year-old woman, naked from the waist up, emaciated, barely breathing. It was explained to us that she was dying of AIDS. We were all in shock. The boys with me instantly became paralyzed. Chan too.

I have thought about this experience a lot. I truly believe this family just wanted us to witness the totality of their family and to witness their daughter, that she lived and that she was loved. It felt difficult to be there, the air was hot and very stale. Lying there was a woman, just a few years younger than me, hoping for a few more breaths. The family didn't think she had much longer. There is a weird thing that happens when the dynamics of a situation play out like this. I have been invited to address congregations at churches just because it probably seemed I was more educated, or dare I say, I had a perceived higher status. I am not sure what to do in those situations, but it happens often enough, and I have always managed to make the best of it. To be grateful for the chance and their trust.

The family was talking to the translator, and I sensed it was coming. When the translator began in English, she asked if one of us would please say something to help their daughter find peace in her transition. All the boys froze even more, but I noticed a softness in Chan. I asked him if he would. This normally defiant, drug-seeking, but truly authentic kid stepped up, took his beanie off, exposing his dreads, and began to speak.

What followed was the most authentic attempt to help comfort and inspire that I have ever seen. Lines of Grateful Dead lyrics and hopes for himself and this woman flowed through Chan, and we all let a few tears slide. I was so damn proud of that kid. The family was grateful too. We all hugged and said our goodbyes to this young woman and walked out of the rickety structure, grateful for the fresh air and for another minute to breathe. We knew she'd pass soon, and we got to witness her and hear about her life.

We also got to see someone find and maintain their authenticity during an incredibly vulnerable situation. Your plans don't automatically mean compromise and doing only what others want you to do. Your plans are an expression of your priorities, and your priorities should stem and flower from your authentic self.

Be you, but work hard at being you. Keep showing up for yourself, for your plans, and your developing authenticity in the process will be a witness to your growth.

So be you, throw in some Grateful Dead lines and theories about the universe in a situation that might not necessarily seem right. Your boldness and work ethic will pull it all together. Chan did, and it was beautiful. In that moment, he straddled the line between expectations and his authenticity perfectly and we all benefited from it. Don't rob the world of your authenticity.

Courtesy of the author

Be Self-Validating

Our relationship with validation is precarious. We all need it, crave it, and find different ways to seek it out. It can become an unhealthy search, and when we don't get it regularly, it can feel like coming off a powerful drug. Validation is intoxicating, and as we talked about while assessing, we should look at our relationship with validation.

I had an unknown and weird relationship with validation growing up (we all do). I got a lot of it growing up from a lot of sources. I was a strong leader and creative, but I always saw myself as the person who quit football too early or as not worthy of validation due to a long list of supposedly horrible things I did as a kid or while growing up.

In 2014 I was getting burned out again. I was in a work situation that demanded a lot from me, and I was teetering on the edge. I was living in paradise; I paddle boarded twice a day and watched the incredible sunsets from my home every day. Yet, I still couldn't avoid the burnout. Somewhat on a whim, I decided to check off the last item on a bucket list I'd made when I graduated from college. I wanted to walk the Camino de Santiago. Five hundred miles across Northern Spain. I convinced a friend to come along and with no training whatsoever and all the wrong equipment, we got on a plane and flew to Madrid.

I have a whole book I want to write on this experience. I have never experienced so much and so many different people and lessons in just thirty-four short days. I almost quit the first day after miles and miles of endless uphill climbs. I stuck with it. My backpack was too small for me. I had packed too much, and I was ridiculously out of shape, but I could sense, even on that difficult first day, that it was what I needed to experience, so I walked on. All the likes on Facebook helped keep the wind at my back, such is the power of validation. At times we won't quit just out of fear that the validation will go away. Again, validation is a weird yet powerful thing.

About ten days into the walk, my legs developed a nasty case of shin splints. Oddly, it was the same injury I used to justify my poor performance in football in high school. I guess I can get them pretty bad. Finally, my shins screamed louder than my ego and I had to stop walking. I was crushed. I was walking with a great group of people, and I didn't want to seem weak and miss out on the walk with my friends.

Enter Jonathan, the man from Northern Europe who had traveled at least a thousand miles from his home with his trusty donkey. Yes, donkey. At the hostel that morning, he encouraged me to rest. He made some tea and sat me down to talk, a chat that would change my life. I guess a lot of time walking with a donkey can teach you a lot.

I think he recognized quickly that I had an unhealthy relationship with validation. He saw how attached I was to the idea of walking every mile of the Camino. We talked for a while. He took a big sip of his tea and told me to close my eyes. He asked me to imagine that on my chest I had a red button and a green button. He continued. He asked me to imagine people, all types of people coming up to me and pressing either my red button or my green button. He told me the red gave me feelings of negative validation while the green button gave me positive validation. As I imagined these people, they became real. I saw friends and family, co-workers and clients. I knew what button they were going to push! It was weird. I saw as he spoke all these people pushing whatever button they chose and then me reacting to the button they pushed. I noticed how many people pushed the red one, making me almost dependent on them. It didn't matter that it was negative. I still wanted the validation.

Jonathan paused, fed his donkey a carrot, and then continued with his exercise. He asked me to think of some important and powerful memories. He asked me about the messages of those memories. He asked which color button would push those memories and messages. As I sifted through a lot of memories and their messages, I realized how often the red button was being pushed.

I told Jonathan.

He asked me if the feelings were different. You know, between the green and red buttons. I sat with his question and realized there wasn't much difference. I still had a strong reaction.

He smiled. Validation is validation, no matter if the source is positive or negative. It will confirm whatever part of you or message you want. Validation is a drug, he said. We can get our fix from others or ourselves but once hooked, we will always need it.

I asked him how I fix this. I didn't like how susceptible I was to validation. The cravings for it, especially when we are stuck, can be so strong. Whether we get that validation from video games or feeling anti-everything, we are still getting validation and seeking and getting validation to ultimately validate whatever messages or lens we want to see the world from. I felt so stuck and hopeless.

He asked me to close my eyes again.

He asked me to bring up a memory, a strong one. I did. He told me I should put myself in that memory as firmly as possible; I did, and it was uncomfortable. He asked me to create a little space between me and the memory, and just like I asked you to do earlier, he asked me to get really clear on its message. I complied. I told him the message. He said he didn't ask me for that. More validation seeking, I guess. He did ask what button the message would press; I said, obviously red.

As we created a little space between me, the memory, and the message, he urged me to find evidence for the message it was giving me and asked if that evidence changed the button it pushed. It did change it. That adult perspective gave the message a more positive meaning. So, I told him that the memory now felt more positive and that it just pushed the green button.

"I didn't ask it to do that."

Jonathan was a kind and very good teacher. I felt like I was in a movie like *Karate Kid*.

Jonathan simply taught me the simple truth that no memory or person should ever push either button. Only you should, and you need to make sure you are the only one who pushes them.

I've tried to live that way ever since. It is very hard; at times it feels impossible. My relationship with validation is a daily negotiation, I don't think anyone is immune to that. But just like learning to wax on and wax off, you are deflecting everyday people's attempts to hit your red or green button. You are taking time and creating a space to choose how to be validated. You become self-validating by doing so.

You ultimately, always, can choose how to see any given situation, advice, comment, or insult. Our relationship with validation directly influences our daily routines and plans. Let life and others hit the red button, and we will give up on our plans but still get validated by doing so. Giving up will still validate you. That line between good and bad validation is razor-thin, but if you can learn to create a little space and then you yourself press the button, then your plans have a good chance of sticking and you have a good chance of pushing the green button more.

Be a Lover of Hard Work

Your plans will require new attempts implementing this new mindset we've been building toward.

These tools and skills we've learned will require work. Unavoidable work.

You being stuck might feel easier to you; hitting that point where your despair matches your hope like mine did in Maui is a pivotal moment for all of us. We make life too easy. Fast food, delivery apps, and streaming services can all combine to keep us stuck in place. The two skills of clear starts and finishes and getting into your body to overcome the mind combine here. Honestly, you can fight me on this, because, trust me, I have fought myself over this, but the mind and the body love hard work. We have a severe lack of it in modern society because we pawn it off onto others. It is a shame and a waste. We are capable of so much more than we can see and believe.

I was in Malawi last summer and there was some hard work involved. As always with projects and coordinating in foreign countries, we had to make many pivots, and on that day the supplies and equipment were running behind schedule. I noticed about a half-dozen women: instead of just standing there, they carried buckets of water on their heads from a well to water individual macadamia nut trees. The walk to each one was long, and I guess I saw an opportunity to get my overweight and old body working again while having the kind of unique shared experience that occurs when you work hard alongside others.

So, I made the walk over to the well and tried to explain that I wanted to help. They were stunned and just laughed. To prove my seriousness, I grabbed the next full bucket and walked with the ladies with the heavy bucket on my head, trying my best not to make a fool of myself nor spill a drop of the precious water. I had no clue what they were talking about as we walked, but I liked to think I was part of the fun gossip being traded. As we waited for each bucket to fill, they laughed and giggled as I waited for my next bucket. Only one time did I completely soak myself, when I stepped into a small divot in the dirt path. They roared, and it was quickly becoming one of the best mornings of my life.

It was also seriously hard work. The top of my head killed me. All the stabilizing muscles in my neck, back, and legs were at work; I guess they hadn't been in a long while. The ladies made me take a mandatory break with them. I guess, as we started communicating in broken English and hand gestures, I had joined their workers' union as well. They made sure I was safe even as the men who were working around us were hooting and hollering about the white dude who was working all morning with women. They had plenty to banter back to the men about. It was all in good fun. It was hot, we all had tasks, and we were working hard. There was a strong sense of community.

By the time lunch came, I was spent. I had made a couple dozen trips balancing a five-gallon bucket of water on my head over uneven terrain. It had felt amazing, and the experience was even better.

Whether you are painting a canvas, computing the hell out of a spreadsheet, styling hair, or framing a house, there is beauty, energy, and camaraderie in working hard. If you let yourself, if you work hard and as you toil eliminate the mental blocks that keep you from working even harder on your plans, you will experience the same feelings I did that morning in Malawi. You will fall in love with hard work.

I studied advertising in college. Tons of group projects. Tons of late nights, just about the same amount of sleepless nights. My fellow group members and I all worked until the sun came up, showered, changed, and then went to present our projects. I loved it. Deadlines, clear starts, and finishes become craveable, if we just let it all unfold and didn't let the lazy in. Those crazy ideas you created on the big poster board will happen if we fall in love with the hard work it will require to make them happen. It won't ever turn out like we imagine, but we will get somewhere new, and that place is usually better then where we currently find ourselves.

Let me drive the point home with one last story.

After high school, remember, I worked in demolition for a pool plastering company. It was hard and exhausting work, but I never felt better. Tons of early mornings while still trying to be social at night. Caffeine and adrenaline were my hard-working companions. We'd show up at the work yard in the morning and get our job assignment for the day. One day, I saw on the docket a pool cleaning in Santa Barbara. We needed to prepare the pool for sandblasting. I was excited. Santa Barbara was over an hour away and a beautiful drive. Pool cleaning seemed easy enough, and that was the only job on the schedule. Easy day!

My buddy and I loaded the truck up with the equipment needed and we took off. We arrived at a sort of run-down house on a bluff. The property was huge and beautiful. I couldn't say the same about the state of the pool. It was partially drained. It was the darkest of green colors and there was probably about two feet of what I was later told was "duck butter." I guess the local ducks and birds used this pool as their personal pool/toilet. It needed to be spotless before sandblasting. So, we grabbed five-gallon buckets, shovels, and wheelbarrows, and we started the task at hand.

I decided early on, when I got hired at this job, that I would do good work. This pool cleaning was a huge challenge to that decision. I didn't let any negative thoughts come up. As we slipped and slid in the duck butter we laughed, cursed ourselves sarcastically, and kept working. The end, a clean pool, was our goal, and we had some time constraints. We both had dates later that evening.

Our boss came all the way up to see us from Los Angeles. He knew what we were up against. When he arrived, he was shocked. Our dump truck was filled with the nastiest of loads. We were tired, smelly, and almost done. He was shocked and impressed. Those are good feelings to create in your boss, in yourself. My friend and I were just in love with the start and finish of it all. We wanted to do good, hard work. Our bodies were responding, and we were happy. Our boss took photos and hollered over his radio that we deserved a bonus for this job.

We drove home exhausted, reeking of duck butter, and wondering if our dates would be ruined because our odor would be too offensive. We didn't care. That finish we had accomplished was worth its weight in gold.

Falling in love with hard work means becoming open to falling in love with clear starts and finishes based on your current priorities and goals. I hope every one of you gets the chance to feel what we did that day and the other such days I've experienced since.

The days when we let our minds take over and dictate our perspective are not ruined, they are salvageable. We did have days working that job when we complained about the heat, the red ants that bit us as we jackhammered, or a job that seemed impossible. Those days were long and overly arduous. Our minds for sure got the better of us and our work suffered; it just wasn't good work. Expect the ups and downs as you implement your plans, but keep at it.

But as you get started on your new plans, be a lover of hard work. Your efforts alone will ensure that your plans stick better.

Be Compassionate

Whether this next statement is controversial or not is up to you. I spoke earlier about service and the need to get out of our own heads and into the community at large, doing something good and not at all focused on yourself. Of course, this process of getting unstuck and moving requires us to be kind and patient with ourselves, but I would also say that to focus solely on yourself, your problems, fears, and anxieties is counterproductive and extremely unhealthy, even if the current narrative in the world is always more therapy, more pills, and less personal accountability. If you can't get your plans going, go find compassion focusing on someone else, or some cause greater than you. Build your compassion muscle, become empathetic and compassionate toward others, and watch your worries and fears slowly melt away. Compassion builds perspective. A perspective I think you will enjoy more than your current state of being. Service is the antidote for over-identifying with your problems.

Jackie

Growing up, a lot of my extended family lived in San Diego. I loved spending time with my cousins down there. I grew up with all girls, so I welcomed the time with my boy cousins playing sports, riding bikes, and just doing boy stuff. My parents would take us to San Diego at least monthly. We'd always get home late. Driving away from my grandparents' home with them waving goodbye to us as we drove away always caused a bunch of tears.

One evening, we arrived back at our home in Los Angeles cranky and tired, and I was being a little brat. I was stuck in all my nine-year-old problems, which at the time felt like the end of the world. My parents probably wanted to send me off to boarding school. I made a big fuss over wanting cooler shoes.

My mom checked our answering machine (this was the eighties, mind you), and a couple of messages played as I was unloading stuff from the minivan. I heard the familiar voice of my mom's friend Jackie.

"Sandy, I'm awfully hungry, I have no food. Call me back, please. Thank you."

I stopped in my year-old Air Jordans. The tone in her voice. Her leaving a voicemail like that. Her being hungry. I just got it that day, even though I was so young. What could I possibly have to complain or worry about? It was all gone. In an instant. Gone and totally pointless. My mom and I went and grabbed some groceries and dropped them off to her at her tiny and desperate apartment.

Listen, it is not like I was never a pain in the ass again. It is not like I never worried again. You've read my stories; I've failed and have been paralyzed as much as I have found success and peace. I have seen plans slip through my hands instead of sticking because I was hyper-focused on myself and my fears. But that night, late, when we dropped off food to Jackie, I felt, just like the Grinch, my heart growing a little bit bigger and my perspective changing by miles. Me not having some want or need fulfilled, or me thinking the world was too tough or against me, melted away. We had a mission, and it took priority. If you are looking for a good start and finish, maybe your first task to attempt should be looking beyond yourself and lifting another.

Of course, I want you to assess and figure out the root causes of your worries and fears—those very present and pressing things that keep you from engaging with your hopes, dreams, and plans. I want you to understand them and keep them in your self-awareness so you can actively combat them. The best way to do that is find new horizons and perspectives through flexing your compassion muscle.

I promise you, the momentum it will create for you will be profound.

Lastly, Be Passionate, about Something, Anything

I have worked hard to make my plans truly stick. Those plans I made on Maui changed the course of my life. I honestly had no clue how taking that hard look at myself would turn out or what kind of life it would turn into. I have had heartaches and moments of overwhelming triumph. At times, a lot of times, I doubted myself to the point of despair. I almost gave up on my plans numerous times. The first couple of years after I made that promise to Jaime on his deathbed, I could have easily given in to my mind. None of it was easy.

Sticking the Landing

On a long, hot drive to Mexicali to pick up some paperwork for my son Carlos's visa, we got into a good conversation about what he might want to study in college. He had no clue. I was still getting to know Carlos on a deeper level. I knew he was a hard worker and loved the details in things, whether it was building Legos or playing soccer. He could be both technical and particular. We talked about these aspects of his and what possibilities they could create for him. He found no passion in being a doctor or lawyer, but when I mentioned that the college where he was accepted had an aviation program, he perked up a bit. We explored the idea without judgment. We were in the creation phase; the sky was the limit. My uncle was a commercial airline pilot and I shared what I knew of his career, life, and his life's trajectory. The idea took root in him. I brought him some books the next time I came down, and soon he was committing to the aviation science major at his university. He devoured aviation books, studied hard, learned English, and received scholarships. He lived and breathed aviation. It wasn't easy for him; he wasn't a natural student at first. The orphanage he grew up in didn't put a huge emphasis on his education. But he put the effort in. He woke up early and studied late. He set his priorities and built strong habits and predictable routines. None of those steps felt boring; the hard work needed didn't diminish his passion for aviation.

Soon he was flying planes and falling in love with real estate investment. He played soccer on a local team and got his driver's license and first car. His first job was cleaning garbage cans at the university, which he loathed, but it led him to another, better job. He started practicing jiu jitsu and dating. Each thing he lent his passion to created more momentum for him. Everyone around him could tell he really truly loved what he invested his time in. Watching him graduate from college and seeing him fly a plane over my head for the first time were very proud moments for me. My passion, since that day in Maui when I set these plans in motion, was his and his brother's success and momentum. As he learned about weather patterns and airport talk, I built businesses, created steadier income streams, and got my life on track after my sabbatical and being burnt-out on all my old messaging.

I truly did start from the ground level. I followed the exact same steps I have outlined here in this book; through trial and error, I found this system that worked.

Life has been truly kind since. Not easy but kind, meaning, I was kinder to myself as I built. I learned impossibly hard lessons; I lost friends to overdose and suicide. Relationships I had built crumbled and opportunities I wanted more than anything slipped through my hands, lost forever. I stayed kind to myself.

And, despite all of that, I still found passion for my plans. I kept moving. Making my bed, relying on my body for hard work and my mind for its creativity. I pivoted and planned all over again. I started and I finished tasks and met my short-term goals. I won my work ethic back.

Passion, not obsessiveness and over-identification, kept the fire going for me and my son Carlos.

It will be the same for you.

Conclusion

MAKE SOME PLANS

Well, we've come to the end, folks. Thanks for bearing with me. This probably felt like a super long coaching session. In all honesty, it was, but probably more so for me.

This may have been an unconventional way of learning about how to make your plans stick, but I hope you've come to know yourself better, and by doing so, are prepared to do a sort of battle with your mindsets and messaging.

To this day, Supergirl continues to teach me; my hiccups and successes do as well. Your failures and mistakes will do the same, but you know yourself and them so much better now, and they don't have to control you anymore.

In Maui, when I started to really assess where I was in life, so many memories came flooding in. Their messages screamed and yelled at me. It was all so negative and distressing. Possibly for the first time, I acknowledged how arrested my development was. All those messages had gained a lot of ground; they had completely stalled me out in some very important aspects of my life.

After assessing, I desperately wanted to feel a state of unarrested development. A state of freedom from stale messages, a new sense of creativity and momentum. So, I wrestled up some kindness, hope, and passion, albeit a small amount, and followed the process I've been rambling on about in this book.

I followed this formula:

1. I assessed the important and the hard concepts that really make us human so I could understand what I was up against. *Assess* is really about getting to know your resistance patterns in their many forms.

2. I gave myself permission to look at everything anew, whether that was my mentors, my third spaces, or my hobbies. We are never truly stuck. Just like that van in Mexico, we just need plans that will actually work, that are based on what we really know about ourselves and where we'd like to go.

3. I took many scary first steps. I got my work ethic in order. I wasn't afraid of hard work. I simply had to do what I brainstormed around. My curiosity around my plans became stronger than my fears. I based myself in the knowledge that I could work hard. The evidence said, no matter what, I could put in the work if I wanted to.

4. Who I was becoming began to matter more than what I did for a living. How people would remember me became more significant for me. I wanted to show up as a good dad and a better human. Understanding the characteristics that are important to you and that you want to be known for adds fuel to the fire of your plans; it adds meaning and keeps the passion for your priorities alive.

There are so many books that will dive into the specifics of goals and habits. There are books that dig deep on the power of our minds and the dangers of technology and certain societal narratives. It can all get really confusing. Even good advice can grow stale. Seek out what interests you, but do me a favor:

Truly try the formula I've guided you through. Follow it. Go through the whole process. Don't judge or cherry-pick. Just practice, deliberately, the steps I laid out. Breathe. Pick yourself up if you stumble. Brush yourself off, but, please, adjust your plans and rededicate yourself to the work of making them stick by working the formula again. It's just more data.

As David Foster Wallace offered at the end of his profound and wonderfully epic graduation speech, *This is Water*, "I wish you more than luck."

I wish you tons of hard work wrestling your new plans into existence, I wish you relief from your old and tired messages, and I wish you a life of unarrested development, peace, and new growth every day.

Make some plans now, believe yourself as you work the formula, and I know you'll stick some good plans.

Courtesy of the author

ACKNOWLEDGMENTS

This book was a battle for me. Juggling my work, managing my ADHD, and trying to distill my journey into a path you all could take with me was no joke. The struggle was real.

Luckily, I have an exceptional family and amazing friends. I have mentors I can call. My agent, Zach Kristensen, who I can bug. And the whole crew at Mango Publishing to thank for getting me to the point where I can put this out into the world and see what comes of it.

I really hope what comes is a lot of plans gaining traction and people working through what is getting in the way of their hopes and dreams.

Work hard, everyone, it is worth it.

REFERENCES

"23 College Dropout Statistics That Will Surprise You" (*creditdonkey.com*): CreditDonkey. "23 College Dropout Statistics That Will Surprise You." www.creditdonkey.com/college-dropout-statistics.html

"New Report Shows Teen Mental Health Worsening" (*Psychology Today*): Psychology Today. "New Report Shows Teen Mental Health Worsening." www.psychologytoday.com/us/blog/the-science-of-self/202303/new-report-shows-teen-mental-health-worsening

"Stats and Facts About College Graduates Unemployment Rate (2022)" (*whattobecome.com*): WhatToBecome. "Stats and Facts About College Graduates Unemployment Rate (2022)." whattobecome.com/blog/college-graduates-unemployment-rate

"17 Essential High School Job Statistics [2023]: How Common Are High School Jobs" (*Zippia*): Zippia. "17 Essential High School Job Statistics [2023]: How Common Are High School Jobs." www.zippia.com/advice/high-school-job-statistics

"23 Alarming High School Dropout Rate Statistics" (*creditdonkey.com*): CreditDonkey. "23 Alarming High School Dropout Rate Statistics." www.creditdonkey.com/high-school-dropout.html

"U.S. daily time spent playing games/computer use by age 2022" (*Statista*): Statista. "U.S. daily time spent playing games/computer use by age 2022." www.statista.com/statistics/502149/average-daily-time-playing-games-and-using-computer-us-by-age

"Average Student Loan Debt: 2024 Statistics" (*BestColleges*): BestColleges. "Average Student Loan Debt: 2024 Statistics." www.bestcolleges. com/research/average-student-loan-debt

"What is the average credit card debt?" (*usatoday.com*): USA Today. "What is the average credit card debt?" www.usatoday.com/money/ blueprint/credit-cards/what-is-the-average-credit-card-debt

Apollo Technical. "17 Remarkable Career Change Statistics To Know (2024)." www.apollotechnical.com/career-change-statistics

ABOUT THE AUTHOR

- In 2004, while in college, Josh co-founded the Kaiizen Foundation serving orphaned and vulnerable children projects worldwide.

- Kaiizen has consistently served over five hundred orphaned and vulnerable children in the US, Mexico, Peru, Brazil, India, South Africa, Nepal, and Eswatini.

- Josh helped found and create Kwahka Indvodza, Eswatini's first male mentoring project, in 2012. It now serves over 10,000 young men every month with various mentoring, training, and educational programs/initiatives.

- Josh now consults for other NGOs and government organizations on male mentoring issues.

- In 2008, Josh created an industry-first humanitarian therapy program to help troubled youth in the USA. Working with treatment centers, Josh planned close to a hundred humanitarian trips across the globe, assisting these youth in learning the value of hard work and gaining key socio-emotional skills, alongside deeper therapeutic interventions.

- Kaiizen has led over 250 humanitarian excursions around the world with over 5,000 volunteers since its founding.

- Since 2013, Josh has maintained his own private life-coaching/mentoring practice serving between thirty-five to forty youths at a time, nationwide. He teaches executive functioning skills and socio-emotional concepts, as well as holding his clients accountable to their goals.

- Josh is a co-author of the *Bang Head Here* book series with Hollie Henderson. Written for parents, the series guides them back to healthier communication and cultures in their homes.

- Josh is the founder and CEO of Able, a technology platform created to learn and practice needed skills for launching well in the world.

- Josh currently consults on a wide variety of businesses and start-ups focused on healthy youth development.

- He's traveled to over seventy countries, has adopted two sons, and loves what he does every day, even though young people can be quite a hassle!

Mango Publishing, established in 2014, publishes an eclectic list of books by diverse authors—both new and established voices—on topics ranging from business, personal growth, women's empowerment, LGBTQ studies, health, and spirituality to history, popular culture, time management, decluttering, lifestyle, mental wellness, aging, and sustainable living. We were named 2019 *and* 2020's #1 fastest growing independent publisher by *Publishers Weekly*. Our success is driven by our main goal, which is to publish high-quality books that will entertain readers as well as make a positive difference in their lives.

Our readers are our most important resource; we value your input, suggestions, and ideas. We'd love to hear from you—after all, we are publishing books for you!

Please stay in touch with us and follow us at:

Facebook: Mango Publishing

Twitter: @MangoPublishing

Instagram: @MangoPublishing

LinkedIn: Mango Publishing

Pinterest: Mango Publishing

Newsletter: mangopublishinggroup.com/newsletter

Join us on Mango's journey to reinvent publishing, one book at a time.